David Lynch
Michael Nelson

St. Anne's of Penetanguishene

Huronia's First Mission

David Dupuis

St. Anne's Parish Building Committee

Published and distributed in Canada by:
St. Anne's Building Committee,
28 Robert St. West,
Penetanguishene, Ont.
L9M 1N2
Ph. 705 549-2560
Fax 705 549-4746

Canadian Cataloguing in Publication Data

Dupuis, David Michael, 1958-
St. Anne's of Penetanguishene, Huronia's First Mission

ISBN 0-9688883-0-5

Back cover painting
"Brébeuf's Vision at Toanché"
by Del Taylor

Front cover photo by Mike Odesse
Text Design: G.H. Graphics, Elmvale, ON

Author photo by Mike Odesse
Printed and bound in Canada

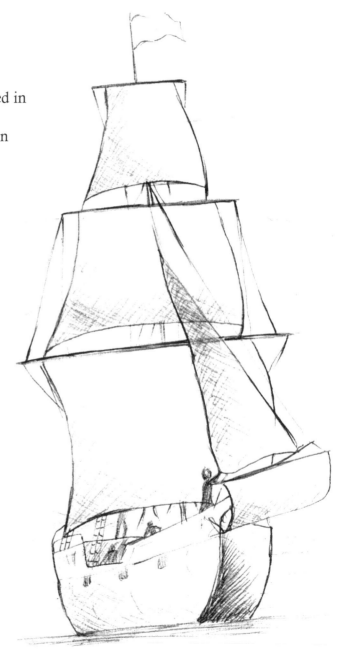

Contents

Acknowledgements

In 1949, Monsignor Jean Marie Castex had the foresight to have a comprehensive history of St. Anne's Parish written. That work, *Along The Bay*, was written and compiled by Mr. E. Davis, a former principal of the Penetanguishene High School, Miss Edith Parker, a public school teacher and Father Frank Sullivan, an assistant at St. Anne's at the time. The booklet was a marvelous resource of facts and has been the cornerstone of this rewritten but expanded history of the parish. It was a godsend of reference and inspiration. I thank the contributors of that booklet for their great effort.

A special thank you to Mrs. Anita Dubeau, our present Mayor and former Chair of the St. Anne's Building Committee, who approached me in the summer of 1999, asking if I would consider writing an updated history of the parish. Anita, thanks for your unfailing support and encouragement for this book project. Thank you as well to your Building Committee: Yvon Gagné, Floyd Putz, Shirley Bellehumeur and Monsignor Leonard O'Malley for its support and enthusiasm. A special thanks to the world's greatest and most supportive editor, my sister, Anne Gagné. Anne, you are always there when I need you! Thank you to you and Yvon for your support and encouragement!

The quality of this book has risen tenfold because of two people. The photographic genius of Mike Odesse, whose beautiful photographs in the colour section has brought out the beauty of the Memorial Church for the first time in ways that only he can. Thanks Mike, for your involvement, cooperation and belief in my project! You are an amazing talent! A special thanks as well to Del Taylor, a fantastic artist whose talents are surpassed only by his generosity and friendship! Del, enough thanks can never be said. Thank you for bringing Pères de Brébeuf and Laboureau to life in pictures and for your exceptional contributions throughout the pages of this book!

Thank you to my third set of editing eyes, a great friend and supporter, Denise Hayes, and my sister-in-law, Roberta "Bobbie" Dupuis. To the following people a great thanks for sharing your thoughts and images of the parish: Henry Bisschop, André Boileau, Père Louis Dignard, Helen Dubeau, Alvin Dupuis, Marcel Duval, Monsignor Leonard O'Malley, Pat Marcille, Père Gerard Pilon, Michelle Quealey, Lucille Robillard, retired Archbishop Leonard J. Wall and Lucille Zoschke. Thanks to Mark Lerman at the Archdiocese of Toronto Archives for his assistance and resources, and the Penetanguishene Centennial Museum for use of its archives and pictures. Thanks again to Pat Gignac and Yvon Gagné for use of their photos!

As always a special thank you to my wife Marlis and children Tanis and Jordan, for putting up with my absences and allowing me to pursue my dream of writing yet another book. Much love always!

__A note to the reader:__
I have attempted to capture the French historical character of the parish and so I have inserted French titles and spellings where applicable in order to maintain the nuances and reality of the parish as it was at its origin. The parish was also originally called "Anne", with an "e" at the end. This was changed over time and so I have reinserted the "e" for historical accuracy. I have applied this rule throughout the text to avoid confusion. Hope you enjoy it! David Dupuis

---

It was with excitement that I read the history of St. Anne's Parish compiled by David Dupuis, illustrated by Del Taylor and photographed by Michael Odesse. I was touched by three things:

1) The Huron Nation was a civilized, peaceful people who received white immigrants into their community;

2) The giant Frenchmen whom we know as the Canadian Martyrs were people of courage in the face of many obstacles such as language, distances and climate. In spite of these, they pursued their mission and remained faithful even in the face of death;

3) Father Théophile Laboureau was another giant Frenchman. He set about to honour the Canadian Martyrs by spearheading the planning, money-raising and building of a church as a memorial to the Canadian Martyrs. St. Anne's Church is as much a monument to his vision as it is to that of the Martyrs.

I am certain that anyone who reads this marvelous piece of history, will be touched by some part of it or all of it.

L. P. O'Malley

Msgr. Leonard P. O'Malley
Pastor

Introduction

In 1615, Joseph LeCaron, the first priest, set foot in the parish that would one day be known as St. Anne's. It was a summer day.

Three hundred and eighty-four years later it is a cold, winter December morning, in the Year of Our Lord 1999 and not a good day to raise new steeples on the church of St. Anne's. The snow and wind blew strong, so strong in fact, that the crane operator and foreman on the job gave thought to postponing the task ahead. Some of the gusts on this December morning reached 50 to 60 kilometers an hour - not a good omen! The crew had delayed a bit, not raising the first one right away, hoping the wind might abate. The rental cost of the huge crane was $250.00 per hour, whether it was used or not. This weighed heavily on the minds of those observers who had gathered to participate in one form or another. But, the delay didn't matter. The winds laughed at the costs and blew mightily.

When it seemed like the winds had abated, the first steeple was raised slowly off the ground by the large crane that towered over 150 feet high. The pastor of St. Anne's, Monsignor Leonard O'Malley, bundled in a parka, watched nervously, as did members of the church fundraising committee; Chair Anita Dubeau, Shirley Bellehumeur, Floydd Putz and Yvon Gagné with his ever-present camera in hand to record the moment for posterity. A small group of parishioners also braved the early winter storm to witness history No doubt had the weather been nicer, the watchful crowd would have been much larger. As the first steeple surpassed the two-third's mark in its ascent, a sudden gust of wind pushed the twenty-foot, two-ton steeple close to the corner front column of the church. Everyone held their breath! The swinging steeple finally steadied, despite the wind, and its journey aloft continued slowly but unabated until it was secure on top of its new perch a few hours later. Still, the wind would not cooperate and the operation to install the second steeple was postponed until the next day.

The next morning dawned cold but sunny without a trace of wind and the second steeple was lifted up into place without a hitch. Finally, 113 years after the commencement of his great dream, the church that Père Théophile Francis Laboureau had begun, was now finished with the steeples that she had always been intended and destined to have. It seemed like she would forever look unfinished, but God in His way must have decided "enough was enough" and sent an anonymous admirer to raise the funds outside of the parish so as to see her finished. This is only but a part of the amazing story that is the parish of St. Anne's of Penetanguishene. It seems that all of her priests, in one manner or another, became enamored with her. Her unparalleled history, location and beauty made her the place of legends.

There can be no doubt, that on the days the steeples of St. Anne's were gloriously raised, Pères de Brébeuf, Lalement and their fellow Martyrs, along with Laboureau, Brunelle, Murray, Brunet, Castex and other late priests who laboured in this parish, must have stood together nearby, watching with pride and affection the work to 'their' church being finished. The miracle of the 'anonymous donor' is a testament to God's ways in this parish, the first parish of Huronia.

A "parish" is a part of an archdiocese that is made up of a church with parishioners or associate members. In this regard, St. Anne's certainly is a parish and then some. The raising of the steeples is a testament to a common vision and plan that is greater than we can ascertain individually, but is attainable as a group and no doubt, with help from above. This is the story of that vision, seen through the wind and the snow, made clearer by time, history and faith. In and throughout life, one must have a little bit of faith. Faith, Hope, Love and Charity are the cornerstones of the Church. With these elements, despite the weather, dreams can come true. The proof is here at St. Anne's!

St. Jean de Brébeuf

I

The Footsteps of Saints

In July of 1608, Samuel de Champlain captained one of three ships owned by Pierre Du Gua de Monts, a wealthy French financier wishing to establish a New World trading monopoly. Sailing from the ancient French seaport of Honfleur, on this his third trip, Champlain established his "Habitation" at "Kébec", an Algonquian place meaning, "where the river narrows".

He survived a near mutiny to have his men construct three two-story dwellings, and a single story warehouse all surrounded by an inner palisade, a moat, drawbridge and outer palisade. He and his 24 men, who included a 16-year-old adventurer named Étienne Brûlé, battened down the hatches to face their first North American winter. By April, only eight remained, and of these, four were still terribly ill. Champlain and Brûlé were amongst those that survived bitter cold,

five-feet-deep snow, scurvy and other diseases.

When, in the spring of 1609, word arrived from France that de Monts expected 'a great harvest' that autumn, Champlain decided to push upstream of the great river, (St. Lawrence), to meet the Indians closer to the interior, near their hunting grounds, in the hope of getting "the pick of the furs".

As the Algonquins usually established their spring fur trading center at the LaChine Rapids, (on the present island of Montreal), Champlain ventured to meet them there. With eleven armed men, he also decided to attack the arch-enemies of the Algonquins, the dreaded Iroquois, whose home territory lay in present day New York State. The Iroquois often attacked the northern tribes on their annual fur trading expeditions before they could be delivered into French hands,

Samuel de Champlain, Governor of New France, greatly admired the Huron nation.

and a counter offensive could help cement ties with their native allies.

Travelling dangerously close to Iroquois territory, Champlain met a camp of Algonquins and Hurons near present day Batiscan. It was his first meeting with "les Hures", an Indian nation whom Jacques Cartier had met 75 years before. Even then, the Huron had been at war with the Iroquois, but by the time of Champlain's first meeting with them, the whole Huron nation had migrated to the Georgian Bay region in a search for peace and security, having tired of the Iroquois war.

The word "Huron" was a name given them by the French derived from the word "hures" meaning "boar" because the Hurons wore their hair in ridges. Actually among the Iroquois and the Algonquins, Hurons were called "Wyandottes" which is the English word for "wendot", a word indicating "someone secluded or living apart". Amongst the Indian nations, the Hurons' home territory, (future Huronia) was known as Wendake. It extended from Lake Simcoe to the Georgian Bay and the French would later estimate it to have a Huron population of some thirty thousand living amongst twenty or so villages.

Champlain would soon learn to respect and value his friendship with this very distinguished and civilized Indian nation of excellent farmers who traded their tobacco, corn and various other produce with other natives in return for furs. They, in turn, would trade the furs to the French in exchange for European wares.

At this first meeting, greetings, presents and smoking rituals introduced friendship. It would later be cemented when Champlain urged and received the aid of 60 of their warriors in a successful raid against the Iroquois. The victory was a great one and feast upon feast marked the occasion. Champlain promised to return the next year to again resume with them their repelling of the Iroquois. This brought great joy and word of his bravery and honour testified to that when he journeyed back to his superiors in France months later. His ships' holds were full of rich furs and a promise of a bright future with his Huron associates.

A painting of Aenons, Chief of Toanché at the time of the first missionaries, addressing his villagers.   *Painting by Del Taylor*

Champlain spent his summers exploring Canada and establishing his "Habitation" and wintered in France, trying to build up French interest in the fledgling colony. In 1610, he arranged for the Huron to take Étienne Brûlé back with them so that Brûlé could learn their ways and explore their region.

In April of 1615, Champlain set sail for New France for the seventh time. With him were four Recollet missionaries, as he felt the natives without religion, were like *"brute beasts...I exerted myself to find some good friars, with zeal, , , to come with me, to plant the faith,"* he would later write. He had such a priest amongst the four in Père Joseph LeCaron.

Assigned to mission amongst the Hurons, LeCaron headed straight to meet them at the LaChine Rapids. So impressed was he with these dignified, tall, handsome natives, that he decided immediately that he would winter with them. He returned to Quebec to briefly gather his things.

On June 19th, Champlain was welcomed like an old friend by the Huron at the LaChine Rapids. Here, he also met an old friend, Étienne Brûlé, who had returned with the Georgian Bay Hurons. Having spent the last four years with them, Brûlé had adapted so well to the native lifestyle and their ways that he almost looked like one of them. The key in Champlain's eyes, was that now Brûlé had a thorough knowledge of the people, their language and territory. His experiences and friendship with the Huron would be immensely helpful to Champlain and New France.

Following up on Champlain's earlier promise to help them in their battle with the Iroquois, the Hurons urged him to help them attack the enemy again. Return with them to Georgian Bay and they would gather a great army of 2,500 warriors, they told him. He agreed, but explained that he would have to first return to Quebec to make the arrangements for the three to four month-long stay, and then, he would return with as many soldiers as he could. Leaving for his 'Habitation' with Étienne Brûlé, he vowed that he would return in four to five days.

On his way to Quebec, they crossed paths with Père LeCaron who was returning to LaChine. Champlain's attempt to persuade the Recollet to return to Quebec for the winter proved futile as the priest was determined to begin his mission. The men parted with the hope that they would rejoin each other in LaChine, for the journey to Huronia.

At LaChine, the natives grew restless after the fifth day when Champlain still hadn't showed. By the eighth day, with still no sign of him, the Hurons had waited long enough. Wondering if Champlain had even made it back to Quebec through hostile Iroquois territory and worried about their own safety, the Huron party began the long trip back to Huronia with Père LeCaron.

The statue of Père Joseph LeCaron, first missionary priest to visit the Hurons at Toanché on Penetanguishene Bay in 1615.
Photo by David Dupuis

3

Two days after the Huron party had left, Champlain's party and ten Hurons arrived at the deserted camp. They then proceeded towards Huronia in an attempt to catch up with the others.

Ever on the alert for signs of the Iroquois, the large birch bark canoes carried the party up the St. Lawrence. Against the often back-breaking current, they paddled. Sometimes they had to push or drag the canoes from shore to shore when rushing waters made paddling impossible. But "frogging" their craft was a pleasure when compared to the long portages when ascending the Ottawa.

By the time they reached Lake Nipissing, the canoes were hundreds of miles apart and Père LeCaron truly felt alone among his native companions. Finally, when the rugged terrain had eased and their journey was too far north for the Iroquois to threaten them, the Hurons in the party relaxed substantially and made congenial colleagues. Ironically, with the hard part of the journey behind them, their villages were still at least 200 miles away.

Seemingly alone, LeCaron huddled at night around the smoldering fire. He prayed for the safety of Champlain and hoped that his own sufferings in this insect-infested land not be in vain. The Hurons in the group sat calmly, their faces covered with animal pelts and mud to stave off the black flies, mosquitoes, sand flies, and insects to which they were accus-

A Huron village called Toanché on the shores of Penetanguishene Bay was the first home of the missionaries in 1615.

tomed. Overcome with fatigue after each arduous day, the good Père often awoke in the morning to find his body covered with insect bites; their accumulated itch and sting often pushed him past the point of endurance.

Dried corn was the only food that the Huron carried on these journeys with the possible exception of a few pounds of deer meat. Even this often became fetid but was usually eaten to the last morsel as they would not stop to hunt, so great was their haste to return home.

After having crossed Lake Nipissing and descended the French River, the party then reached the turbulent waters of Lake Huron, "The Freshwater Sea" as Champlain would later call it. Down along the Georgian Bay, inside of Manitoulin Island, they pushed another hundred miles along the inner channel of the 30,000 Islands. At the north end of what is now Georgian Bay Islands National Park, they began bouncing their way across a small section of rough open water called "The Gap" today, due to an unbroken sweep by the prevalent west winds along the mainland. Finally, the party wound its way into what is now known as Penetanguishene Bay and paddled to shore on the right at "Toanché" or "Atouacha", a Huron word meaning, "one" and "two landing place" respectively. They were home! LeCaron gazed along the shore and saw that the sands here were very white and clean.

The welcome they received at Toanché was second to none, though surely the site of the "black robe" must have been unsettling. As he disembarked from the canoe, Père LeCaron became the first priest to not only set foot in the parish, but be this far west. They walked the path through the dense bush up a small embankment to the village, which was pallisaded and situated near a small creek.

After his landing, Père LeCaron set about acquainting himself with the Indians and observed the people—their character, behaviour, superstitions and attitude towards Christianity. During this initial stay in Huronia, this was all he could accomplish, plus attempt to learn the language reasonably well. No small feat!

Several days later, on August 4th, Champlain's party arrived at Toanché, where he officially laid claim of the land in the name of the King of France by planting a cross at the water's edge. Having just travelled through the beautiful but rugged Georgian Bay landscape, he would later write that he found the hills and terrain around Penetanguishene Bay to be more agreeable:

"Here we found a great change in the country," he wrote," *this part being very fine, mostly cleared with many hills and several streams, which makes it an agreeable district. It seemed to me very pleasant in contrast to such a bad country as that through which we had just come."*

The day after his arrival, Champlain's party walked to the village of Camaron, near present day Sawlog Bay, where a great feast of squash, fish and corn was held in their honour. They returned to Toanché for the night. The day after, they visited two other Huron villages, Touaguainchain and Ossassane, where they were treated to another great feast of corn bread.

On the third day after their arrival, the full party was escorted to Carhagwa by hundreds of Huron for a big celebration, where a relieved and surprised LeCaron greeted him. Amidst great festivities, this Big White Chief was made welcome at Carhagwa, a major village seven miles inland from Toanché. It was an imposing sight, surrounded by a huge palisade 36 feet high with a thickness of three logs—hence the name Carhagwa (the great palisaded fortress).

It was here at Carhagwa, on August 12th, 1615, in the presence of the Governor of New France, Père LeCaron celebrated the first Mass west of Quebec. Brûlé, who surely was present at this event, would have been unmoved. As the first "coureur de bois", he had engrained himself in the native ways and despite wearing a "Lamb of God" medal around his neck, was known to have his way with the native women. The missionaries referred to him as an untrustworthy character - *"an infamous wretch"* as Brébeuf would later call him. Yet, despite his immoral behaviour, there is no doubt that he was instrumental in teaching LeCaron, Champlain and the other Europeans the difficult language and introduced them to the ways of the Huron.

Etienne Brûlé, first European to live among the Huron of this region, was instrumental in forging ties with them, and paved the way for the early missionaries and Champlain's visit here in 1615.

To Champlain, the Huron were remarkable natives with their palisaded villages, toiled fields of corn, squash, beans and tobacco, and crowds of men, women and children who treated him like a celebrity. Besides being experienced farmers, these Huron, the most powerful native nation above the Great Lakes, were skilled diplomats and courageous warriors. Champlain's presence among them was to include an all-out attack on their arch rivals, the Iroquois, south of Lake Ontario. As the Huron gathered a war party the rest of that summer, Brûlé escorted Champlain to all of the Huron villages where great feasts of corn, bread and fish were held to celebrate the great white chief.

The Huron decided to enlist the help of their allies, the Susquehannah tribe in present-day Pennsylvania. Fierce warri-

ors, they were bitter enemies of the Iroquois. Together the Huron and Susquehannah would surely smash the Iroquois! On September 8th, Brûlé was sent with the twelve bravest Huron men through Iroquois land to get to the Susquehannah territory to arrange this. The date of battle was set for October 11th, when they would meet together near the Iroquois stronghold.

With the help of the great Huron chief named Atironta, Champlain spent the rest of that summer gathering 500 Huron warriors, (not the 2,500 that he had been promised earlier) and then they left, for what was expected to be certain victory.

Capturing a small band of Iroquois along the way, Brûlé and his party had been given a hero's welcome at the Susquehannah capital of Carantouan. Frenzied dances and feasts followed one after another, and Brûlé was unable to quickly mobilize the great force that was immediately needed for the fateful rendezvous. Delays ensued when finally a great council approved 500 warriors but this was still delayed as they were slowly assembled. They left late on their three-day journey.

Champlain and the Huron war party of 500 crossed Lake Ontario by canoe and hid them by the water's edge. After a four-day walk in single file, they arrived at the rendezvous place alone. While waiting, the Huron were discovered by the Iroquois, forcing an attack the next day, on October 9th. The element of surprise was gone and the Huron fought as an undisciplined mob. Champlain incurred an arrow injury in his knee and two chiefs were wounded as well. Injured and frustrated, the Huron war party waited seven days, until October 16th. When Brûlé and the Susquehannah failed to arrive, the dispirited attackers returned to Huronia. Brûlé and his tardy war party arrived two days later, assessed the failed Huron attack and quickly returned to the Susquehannah capital, where he stayed the remainder of the winter.

In the spring of 1616, the Susquehannah provided six braves to return Brûlé to Huronia. En route they would be ambushed by an Iroquois war party where Brûlé would flee

This famous painting shows Champlain sending Brûlé and 12 Huron warriors, on September 8th, 1615, to enlist the help of the Susquehannah Indian nation near present day Pennsylvannia.

through the bush. After a few days of wandering, he met three Iroquois and he spoke to them in their language, attempting to befriend them. He returned to their village with them but his attempts at friendship were suspect and they tortured him.

He was subjected to beatings, jumping over fires and to shake hands in such a manner that his fingernails were pulled out. They burned him with fire and pulled out his beard. When one of the Iroquois attempted to pull his Lamb of God medal from around his neck, Brûlé warned him that if he touched it, God would be angry. Watching the threatening black clouds that were forming, he warned that to touch the medal would invoke The Great Spirit's wrath. When the attempt to touch happened again, the storm broke and the Iroquois fled. The Iroquois chief took Brûlé to his cabin, nursed his wounds and thereafter treated him like one of theirs. When Brûlé returned to the Bear tribe at Toanché in 1617, he was guided for four days by a group of Iroquois.

That summer and through the winter of 1615-16, Père LeCaron studied the Huron but found hard toil for converts among the Indians. He discussed with Champlain plans for the future work in Huronia. Many more missionaries would be needed to return here to spread the word of God. In the spring of 1616, they returned to Quebec with the trading parties of the Huron. It was to be Champlain's only visit.

When Champlain next saw Brûlé at Trois-Rivières in the spring of 1618, the leader demanded an explanation as to what had happened to him at the planned Iroquois battle. With his mangled hands and explanation, Champlain's anger quickly passed and he would later write that Brûlé was *"more to be pitied than blamed"*.

Nine years would elapse before Père LeCaron's vision of more permanent missionaries took place. In 1623, he and Father Nicolas Viel returned to Huronia to continue their arduous task accompanied

The early Récollet and Jesuit missionaries of Huronia often toiled alone in harsh conditions and in an atmosphere of mistrust. *Photo by Pat Gignac*

by a Frère Sagard who became their helpmate and chronicler of this period in the attempted converting of the Indians. Finally, a chieftain named Awindaon, a man of 75, asked Frère Sagard for Baptism. Frère Sagard informed the man that he could not until the chief dispensed with his several wives and "superstitious practices". It was clear proof that the missionary road ahead would be bumpy.

In 1624, Père Viel was left alone in Huronia. His congregation consisted of one man and his daughter. By 1625, Père Viel had other native converts among whom, a native named Ahauntsic, was the most fervent. Still, a classic example of the atmosphere of mistrust in which the Black-Robes lived was exemplified that June of 1625. Amidst a large expedition, Viel left Huronia to go to Montreal and to Quebec.

He never arrived but his belongings did.

In 1626, the Recollet asked the Fathers of the Society of Jesus also known as the Jesuits, to continue the missionary work that their order had begun. As a result, on July 25th of that same year, the tall giant Père Jean de Brébeuf along with another Jesuit, Père Anne de Nouë and a Recollet, Père Joseph de la Roche D'Ailon set out for Huronia. The trip was not an easy one. Brébeuf would count 35 portages around rapids and 50 times they were forced to wade into water to push and pull their canoes. Many times they would have to help carry the canoes and belongings several miles through thick bush and rough terrain. Arriving at Toanché in late summer spent and exhausted, as were their native guides, they began their missionary work on the shores of Penetanguishene Bay. Their home was a bark cabin on the outskirts of Toanché which they named the St. Nicolas Mission. In 1626, Brébeuf found himself alone in Huronia and for three years he was the Missionary Pastor of Penetanguishene.

When David Kirke of the British captured Quebec with the aid of the treacherous Brûlé in 1628, Champlain was indignant towards his interpreter. In 1629, Brébeuf left Huronia to return to France due to land transfers between France and England. Having had little success in achieving converts, Père Charles Lalement would remark to him: *"In all things there must be a beginning."*

Word of Brûlé's behaviour took years to reach the Huron of Toanché and when it did, they were not impressed. With the French and Champlain again regaining control of New France in 1633, the stage was set not only for the missions to resume, but Brûlé's fate amongst his friends was sealed as well. Wishing to maintain good trading relations with the great Champlain, the Huron turned on Brûlé, torturing then killing him. His body was then cut up, placed in a pot and cooked. The first and only cannibal feast in Ontario took place that spring day by the shores of Penetanguishene Bay.

That winter, a smallpox epidemic swept through the village of Toanché killing half of its inhabitants. The natives set fire to their longhouses in an attempt to halt the dreaded disease. The smoke apparently formed a ghostly shape above the village which they believed was either Brûlé's spirit or that of his sister, seeking revenge. In a panic, they abandoned the village and it burned to the ground.

Brébeuf, or "Echon" meaning "beautiful tree" as the Hurons had dubbed him, returned again to the land of the Huron, this time with Pères Antoine Daniel and Ambroise Davost and other Frenchmen. Again the trip was not easy, and as always risky. The canoes were soon separated and later Davost's Huron guides stole his baggage and threw some of the priest's books and writing materials into the river. Left to fend for himself, Algonquin Indians helped him find his way to Huronia, spent and exhausted. Daniel too

Etienne Brûlé, first white man to live at Toanché and see Lake Ontario, was killed by the Huron of Toanché on the shores of Penetanguishene Bay for his betraying and lustful character.

Huron guides in Brébeuf's party mysteriously abandoned him despite his pleas and set off for their respected villages. Walking through the dense bush that was so familiar to him, he was astonished to find that Toanché was no longer there.

Of this excursion he touchingly wrote:

"With tenderness and emotion I passed along the place where we had lived…now turned into a fine field and also the site of the old village, where, except for one cabin, nothing remained but the ruins of the others. I saw likewise the spot where poor Etienne Brûlé was barbarously and traitorously murdered…"

Kneeling to give thanks to God for his safe arrival, despite the difficulties, he rose to ponder his course of action. Hiding his baggage in the woods, he set out to find Ihonitiria, just north of Toanché, which he found later that evening. Emerging from a clearing, a cry went out: *"Echon has returned!"* A crowd went out to greet him and

he was given a great welcome and the hospitality of Awindoay, Ihonitiria's most distinguished villager. Here Brébeuf waited and prayed for the safe arrival of his companions.

The other priests and companions eventually arrived, much to Brébeuf's relief, and he escorted them to Ihonitiria. Plans to establish themselves at Ossossane, the largest and most important Huron village were changed, as Brébeuf thought the friendliness and hospitality they had received at this northern village boded well to establish their mission here.

As was custom, the host Huron village and the nearby village of Wenriot came together to build them a new home. Their Huron "longhouse" was 20 feet wide and 36 feet long, its exterior of typical overlapping bark covered over arched poles. Yet the interior was very European, as the priests divided into it into three rooms; the first was an ante/ storage room, the second and largest, a

The beautiful, historic shoreline of Toanché on Penetanguishene Bay. Touched by *greatness*.
Photo by David Dupuis

The Huron palisaded village contained many longhouses which were a marvel of construction and housed several families in each.
Photo by Pat Gignac

was deserted but was able to fit into one of the other canoes which came up behind. One Frenchman named Martin was robbed and abandoned among the Nipissings and one named Baron was robbed and abandoned just as they reached Huronia.

Thirty days after leaving Trois-Rivières, Brébeuf was the first to arrive at Toanché on August 5th, 1634. As soon as they landed, the combination kitchen, dining room, workshop, instruction room and bedroom while the third was the chapel. Their new home would turn out to be a busy place.

On September 11th, 1636, Père Isaac Jogues arrived at Ihonitiria. By 1638, Brébeuf and a Père Chamonot were stationed in the village of Téanaostayé. More missionaries were coming to the area but still the conversion of the Hurons was not easy. Blamed for illnesses, European epidemics which reduced the Huron numbers substantially, and crop failures, "the Black Robes" and their lay helpers or "donnés", were beaten regularly. Due to mistrust, their lives seemed to always hang on the edge, a fate they freely accepted. And there was always the threat of the dreaded Iroquois to the south and their marauding parties.

With satellite missions set up all over Huronia beside Huron villages, it was decided to establish a larger, more permanent mission headquarters. Père Jogues was initially put in charge of overseeing construction of Sainte-Marie (Among the Hurons) which was begun in 1639, near present-day Midland. The first building housed a small chapel, living quarters and a store room. This palisaded settlement would grow to have a blacksmith and carpenter shop, a hospital, cemetery, church and Huron quarters.

A chronicle of the lives of the eight North American Martyrs is important in order to provide insight as to the mettle of these brave Christian pioneers who gave their lives for their faith.

Saint René Goupil

In early spring of 1642, a donné by the name of René Goupil came to Huronia, after having spent two years at the mission of St. Joseph de Sillery near Quebec. Born on May 13, 1608, in Saint Martin, France, this young doctor decided to be a Jesuit at the late age of 30 but had to abandon his studies after only a year as he was deaf. Goupil had not been here long when he accompanied Père Jogues and a party of canoes back to Quebec to return the gravely ill Père Raymbaut in June of 1642.

Leaving Trois-Rivières on August 1, 1642 for the return trip, they were ambushed by the Iroquois on the second day and Jogues and Goupil were taken prisoner. They were escorted to the Iroquois village of Ossernenon in present day New York State and kept captive for weeks. During this time, they were tortured and beaten with clubs. Jogues would later relate that René's face had at one point been beaten so badly that he could only see the whites of his eyes. Their fingernails were torn away and their fingers crunched and chewed to the bones.

In September 29, 1642, after having been allowed outside of the compound to pray with Père Jogues, Goupil was told to return inside. At the gate, a young warrior pulled out a hatchet and sliced the donné on the head. Falling face down, Goupil was mortally struck twice more. Father Jogues bent and gave his friend, whom it is said he loved almost like a son, a final absolution before the lay missionary took his last breath. René Goupil was thus the first of the Martyrs to lose his life.

Saint René Goupil.
Martyred in present day New York State on September 29th, 1642.

Saint Isaac Jogues

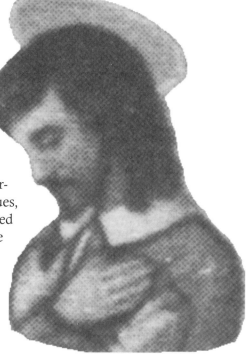

Saint Isaac Jogues.
Martyred in present day New York State on October 18th, 1646.

For unknown reasons, Jogues' life was spared long enough for him to escape with the help of the Dutch in November of 1643. He reached France on Christmas Day. Though his hands had been badly mutilated, Pope Urban VIII readily granted this "Martyr" as he called him, special permission to continue to celebrate Mass. By the next July, Jogues was back in New France. Having heard that the Iroquois now desired peace, Jogues was dispatched with another donné, Jean de la Lande, to Mohawk territory.

It must have been unsettling for him to return to Ossernenon but he did so willingly. He must have often thought back to his youth. Born into a wealthy family in Orléans, France on January 10th, 1607, he had renounced all of this to begin theological studies for the priesthood in 1634. For some unknown reason, he had asked special permission for his ordination to be expedited, which was granted. The call of the Huron missions mysteriously beckoned him.

Now, upon his arrival in Iroquois territory in September of 1646, he found rampant disease and crop failures, not good omens for a Black Robe and his donné helper. In this atmosphere of mistrust, Jogues was invited to lunch in a neighbouring hut. Accepting willingly, he bent through the hut's doorway to enter. It was here that a hatchet mortally struck him on the head. His head was scalped, cut off and his body flung into a nearby river. The date was October 18th, 1646. He became the second of the eight Martyrs.

Saint Jean de la Lande

Jean de la Lande must have wondered what fate awaited him. Dieppe, France, where he was born around 1608, must surely have seemed so far away. Yet the call of service to God had found him in New France in 1642, where he assisted Père Anne de Noüe for four years at the residence at Trois-Rivières until September, 1646.

As the only European to accompany Jogues to this hostile territory, he now found himself alone. On the morning of October 19th, 1646, a day after the martyrdom of his companion Jogues, Jean de la Lande was dragged out to a nearby field outside of Ossernenon. Stripped of his clothes, he was mercilessly tortured for hours. Finally, he was killed, beheaded and his body dumped into a nearby river as well. The third seed of the Martyrs had been planted.

Saint Jean de la Lande.
Martyred in present day New York State on October 19th, 1646

Saint Antoine Daniel

Born in Dieppe, France on May 24th, 1601, Antoine Daniel had begun studies as a lawyer until he received the call of God. In 1629, he was ordained a priest. The call of the Huron missions touched him as well and he found himself in Quebec in 1633 studying the Huron language under Jean de Brébeuf. He picked up the difficult, complex language very quickly and translated the Lord's Prayer, the Creed and others into Huron. Recognizing his gifts, a plan was devised for Père Daniel to transport some Huron children back to Quebec for schooling under him. The plan was abandoned though as the Huron children proved too undisciplined to adapt to the European ways.

When he returned to Huronia in 1638, he relieved Père Brébeuf at Téanaostayé. Over the next ten years, Père Daniel moved between the mission here and Cahiague, near present day Orillia. In June of 1648, while on retreat to pray at St. Marie, he became aware of impending danger and spoke prophetically of death. He confessed and seemed pre-

Saint Antoine Daniel.
Martyred at Téanostayé near Hillsdale on July 4th, 1648.

pared to face the dangers as he returned to Téanaostayé. On July 4th, 1648 with most of the Huron men gone to Quebec for the annual trade, the Iroquois attacked the village. Having just finished saying Mass, Daniel still in vestments, hurried about the village urging the women and children to flee and set about baptizing the injured and dying.

Returning to his church, he was met by the enemy in the doorway. He faced them with a steely gaze, which seemed to momentarily freeze his attackers, giving many Huron valuable minutes to escape. Finally, musket shots and arrows flew toward the lone figure and Père Antoine Daniel, mortally wounded, slumped to the ground and died.

Nonetheless his killers could not resist beating and slashing his body about. Their rage finally satisfied, they set flames to his church and threw his body into it. Their preoccupation with the priest's body had enabled many more Huron to escape. And so this fourth Holy Martyr directly saved many Huron souls.

Saint Jean de Brébeuf.
Martyred at Ste. Ignace near
Waubaushene on March 16th, 1649.

Saints Jean de Brébeuf and Gabriel Lalement

Père Jean de Brébeuf, the most well-known of all the Martyrs, was born in Normandy, France on March 25th, 1593. Poor health sped up his ordination to the priest-hood in 1617. Arriving in New France in 1625, he studied the ways of the Montagnais Algonquins near Quebec City until he left for Huronia in the spring of 1626. After a brief respite in Quebec, the tall Jesuit made his third visit to the land of the Huron in September of 1644.

It was now finally, during these final few years, that the Huron were starting to convert to Catholicism in great numbers. It was in this atmosphere of success that Père Gabriel Lalement arrived in Huronia in August of 1648. Born in Paris on October 10th, 1610, he was ordained to the priesthood in 1638. A professor of Philosophy at Moulins and later, Prefect at LaFlèche College, the call of the missions beckoned to him like it had his two uncles, Charles and Jérome, who headed the missions in New France. Attempting to keep him safe in and around Quebec, his uncle finally relented to Gabriel's appeals to go to the land of the Huron. He studied the Huron language at Ossossane, picking it up quickly and was then assigned to aid Père Brébeuf at the mission of St. Louis in February of 1649. Their collaboration would last only a month.

The work of the missionaries was just beginning to bear fruit when Iroquois war cries were heard on Tuesday, March 16th. Twelve hundred Iroquois quickly captured the village of St. Ignace. Three Huron managed to escape and ran to warn St. Louis of impending danger. Immediately, the old, the sick, women and children fled. Eighty warriors stayed to fight. Brébeuf and Lalement were amongst them to encourage, baptize and hear their confessions. The Huron defended themselves gallantly until on the third assault, they were overwhelmed. Seizing the village, the Iroquois snared the two priests and returned triumphantly back to St. Ignace.

Saint Gabriel Lalement.
Martyred at St. Ignace near
Waubaushene on March 17th, 1649.

An early painting showing the deaths of all eight Martyrs with the
death of Brébeuf and Lalement prominent in the right foreground.

They were dragged to the center of the village where they were tied to two poles. They were mockingly baptized with boiling water and a necklace of red-hot hatchets was placed around their necks. They were beaten profusely, their skin ripped away from their bodies. They were mutilated as burning coals were fastened to their bodies and shoved into their eye sockets. Fire burned at their feet. Brébeuf's withstanding of his torture with emotionless silence further amazed and enraged his captors. Finally, the gentle giant was freed of his suffering, when he died at four o'clock that afternoon.

Gabriel, the more frail of the two, had to endure his suffering the rest of that day and throughout the night. With his now sightless eyes, he gazed heavenward, clasping his hands in silent prayer. Finally, the next morning at nine, the Iroquois grew tired of the torture and ended the small Jesuit's life with a hatchet blow over his left ear. Two days later, seven Frenchmen went to an abandoned St. Ignace and retrieved the bodies of the two Martyrs. Their bones, deemed sacred relics, were reverently cleaned, wrapped and transported back to Quebec. Their bodies were buried together in a simple coffin at Sainte Marie on Sunday, March 21st, 1649.

the next five years at Téanaostaye, St. Joseph's Mission. In 1647, he was sent back to the Tobacco Nation to manage the St. Jean Mission at Etharita, near present day Collingwood.

For two years, he enjoyed great success there. His little mission flourished and grew. Finally, the impending threat of the Iroquois came to pass as they invaded the mission on December 7th, 1649, at three o'clock in the afternoon. Amid cries of horror and slaughter, Père Garnier ran about, helping, baptizing and giving final absolution to dying converts. Despite being shot twice in the stomach and bleeding profusely, Garnier continued to drag himself about, doing his last priestly duties. This further enraged the invaders and two hatchet blows to the head only feet from his beloved chapel ended the life of the seventh Martyr.

Saint Noël Chabanel

The most tragic soul of the Martyrs was Noël Chabanel. Born in Sagues, France on February 2nd, 1613, he began studies for the priesthood at the age of 17 in 1630, and was sent off to New France in 1643. A strong vocation for missionary work had him arriving in Huronia on September 7th, 1644. Though he was a strong linguist, he could not learn the complicated Huron language, which brought on scorn and ridicule from the Huron. He did not adjust to mission life well at all. Native food so appalled him that he often went without, and as a consequence often suffered from lack of nutrition. Though a timid personality, lost and seemingly unhappy, he never abandoned his faith or his zeal for missionary work.

In 1649, he was sent to assist Père Charles Garnier at the St. Jean Mission. When the Iroquois attacked Sainte Marie, she was torched by her builders, rather than let her fall into the hands of the dreaded Iroquois. The priests and Hurons then fled their burning home and escaped to establish Sainte Marie II on what is now called Christian Island. Père Noël Chabanel was then quickly reassigned to help the new mission on the island and he left Père Garnier just hours before the Iroquois swarmed down on St. Jean and Père Garnier.

Saint Charles Garnier.
Martyred at Etharita near Collingwood
on December 7th, 1649.

Saint Charles Garnier

This priest was born in Paris on May 25th, 1605 and ordained in 1635. The call of the Georgian Bay missions had him arriving in Quebec in June of 1636 and in Huronia only a month later. He spent 1639 and 1640 with the Tobacco tribe in the east before being assigned for

Saint Noël Chabanel.
Martyred near present day Wasaga Beach
on December 8th, 1649.

After a safe but harsh winter at Sainte Marie II on what is today called Christian Island, the remaining Huron and the Jesuits retreated forever back to Quebec in the spring of 1650. A chapter in the nation's and the parish's history was irrevocably closed. The missions of Huronia were no more. Or were they?

That night, as he knelt in silent prayer, he heard the cry of the Iroquois and woke his Huron guides who fled in panic. Unable to keep up with them through the night, he collapsed from exhaustion, where he arose the next morning to continue alone. That day, December 8th, 1649, he came across an errant Huron by the Nottawasaga River. Blaming the Black Robes for all their difficulties, the Huron renounced the priest, hatched him to death and threw his body into the river. He was the last of the eight Martyrs to give up his life to spread the Faith.

The 1ˢᵗ Lieutenant-Governor of Upper
Canada - John Graves Simcoe

2

The Establishment of Penetanguishene

The conquering Iroquois mysteriously receded back to their land in the future United States after their vicious victory of 1649. Wandering bands of Ojibway sparsely settled into the area but they did nothing to truly occupy it with their presence like the Huron before them. For the next one hundred and fifty odd years, while New France passed into the hands of the British, the great vast land of Huronia lay empty.

In the 1770s, the United States declared its independence from Britain during its revolution. British colonies here in Canada resisted American invasions that attempted to forcibly persuade them to join their union. In 1791, Quebec was divided in two. The oldest French inhabited section to the east became Lower Canada and the western portion up the Saint Lawrence was renamed Upper Canada.

For years, mistrust loomed between Britain and the United States. Border skirmishes were frequent with North-West Company trading ships being frequently seized by Americans and vice versa. Upper Canada's first Lieutenant Governor, John Graves Simcoe quickly chose Fort York (Toronto) as his Capital in the summer of 1793. Then he turned his attention to finding a more secure western trade route by exploring the Great Lakes region that same Fall. Into Lake Huron and down the north shore of Georgian Bay, Simcoe's flotilla of five canoes landed on what is now known as Georgian Bay Island's National Park.

A fierce wind and high waves kept him on the island but through his scope, he saw the entrance to Penetanguishene Bay. With its long, protected, narrow harbour and high rising hills, he quickly

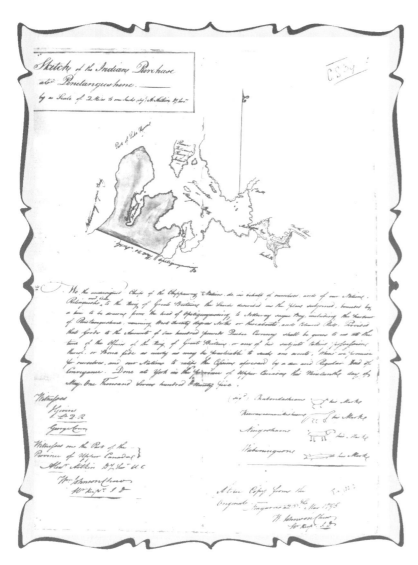

The document of land purchase of the Penetanguishene Peninsula and abutting lands and islands signed by four Ojibwa Chiefs on May 22nd, 1798.

saw its military advantages and chose it as an ideal site on which to build a fort. With him was Deputy-Provincial Surveyor Alexander Aitken, whose initial survey and instant report urged building operations to begin without delay. On December 20th, 1794 his report to the Privy Council stated:

"Penetanguishene bids fair to become the most considerable town in Upper Canada as the passage to the Northwest will be established here."

It wasn't until May 22nd, 1798, four years later, that the vast land around Penetanguishene Bay, as well as the islands later named Hope, Christian and Beckwith were purchased for 100 pounds. The sale was solidified with the signature of four Ojibway chiefs.

It was all part of the preparations for war under the administration of the new Lieutenant-Governor of Upper Canada, Francis Gore. When Gore went on leave to Britain in 1811, the administration of the fledgling colony was left in the capable hands of Major-General Isaac Brock, Commander of the combined forces of Upper Canada. It was Brock who had shrewdly masterminded the preparations for war as hostilities

between Britain and the United States escalated. He had heard the words of the American President Thomas Jefferson who stated, the invasion of Canada would be "*a mere matter of marching!*" How could it be otherwise, the Americans thought. The U.S. had a population of 8 million and the two Canada's a mere 300,000 inhabitants, most of them being former Americans wishing to maintain ties to Great Britain. Surely there would be minor resistance! But when on June 18th, 1812 the United States declared a state of war, Upper Canada's Brock was ready.

Where Lake Michigan joins Lake Huron at the island of Michilimackinac, a small group of British soldiers and voyageurs had been stationed for several years. Then in 1796, Michilimackinac was conceded to the United States. The small British garrison was transferred to St. Joseph's Island. It was from this fort and blockhouses that one hundred and eighty voyageurs and thirty British regulars plus seventy painted birch bark canoes with almost three hundred tribesmen set out to re-capture Michilimackinac the night of July 16, 1812. Their surprise attack, ordered by Brock at the start of the war, was bloodless and successful, especially since the Americans on the island were not yet aware that they were at war.

The War of 1812 raged on and it wasn't until seventeen months later, December 3rd, 1813, that the Secretary of State, the Earl of Bathurst, gave orders to proceed in Penetanguishene with the building of blockhouses, vessels, defences and whatever was necessary *"to meet the enemy!"* Commander "Tiger" Dunlop and his 89th Regiment cut the first crude trail here from Kempenfelt Bay in November of 1814. At this same time Colonel George Head was dispatched from England to command the fledgling post here. By the time he arrived on February 29th, 1815 and moved into his cabin a week later, it was all for naught. Peace had been obtained with the Treaty of Ghent on Christmas Eve, two months earlier. Head was to return to Kempenfelt Bay to await further orders. Penetanguishene was no longer a priority.

The Naval Establishments at Penetanguishene occupied a quarter of a mile along the waterfront between 1817 and 1820 and housed the 68th Regiment.   *Photo by Pat Gignac.*

The Treaty of Ghent signed by British and American representatives on December 24th, 1814, brought an end to the War of 1812.

With thoughts of impending American invasion never far from their minds, the British Admiralty decided to move back to Penetanguishene in July of 1816, despite the peace. From the Nottawasaga River, supplies were transported by the three forty foot, forty ton Durham ships based here called the "Mosquito", "Wasp" and the "Bee". Between 1817 and 1820, the Establishment grew over a quarter of a mile along the waterfront, as buildings were constructed to house the 47 naval personnel and 27 officers and soldiers of the 68th Regiment. Munitions were stored on Beaver Island, later called Magazine Island and a large, three story, red storehouse was constructed near the water's edge, by the main wharf. Easily the most imposing and impressive building on site, the storehouse was most vital, as it housed the supplies for the base: 10 foot stacks of clothing bales, miles of rope and rigging, sails, hundreds of barrels of salt pork, food stores, armaments and various other supplies.

After the Rush-Bagot Arms Limitation Treaty between Canada and the United States was signed, two seventy-foot schooners, the "Newash" and the "Tecumseth" were immediately decommissioned here and kept "in ordinary" without masts or rigging. They eventually sank in the bay. Two American warships captured in the summer of 1814, the "Tigress" and the "Scorpion", were also kept here and eventually rotted and sank in the waters off Magazine Island.

The Treaty of Ghent had also re-established boundaries between the two countries thus Drummond Island was to be turned over to the Americans by 1828. The detachment that had moved there from Michilimackinac at war's end was now ordered moved to Penetanguishene. Any civilian whose loyalty sided with Britain was offered free land. Between 1818 and 1828, all of the British soldiers, many of the fur traders, and quite a number of Métis and Indians began the move here to this location.

The government hired a brig named "Wellington" and a schooner captained by a man named Flackett to convey the troops, Indians and stores to the new post. Lieutenant Carson was the Commander of the 68th Regiment with Mr. Keating as Adjutant and Sergeant Rawson as the Barracks Master. It was the sorry duty of Sergeant Rawson to lower the British flag on Drummond Island while Lieutenant Carson surrendered the keys to the United States authorities.

The Wellington landed at Penetanguishene in November, 1828, but the schooner, named "Hackett" (Alice) would not be so lucky. On that fatal trip, Hackett was laden with a detachment of soldiers and their military supplies, a French Canadian named Lepine with his wife and child and a tavern keeper named Fraser with thirteen barrels of whiskey. Also on board was Ezechiel Solomon, whose property consisted of two horses, four cows, twelve sheep, eight hogs, harnesses and household furniture.

Between Drummond Island and Manitoulin Island much of the whiskey was consumed while the ship sailed into a storm. The crew and soldiers were much too inebriated and soon, the schooner was riding the crest of a rock. Mrs. Lepine, unable to make shore with her child, wrapped him in a blanket, tied him to her back and then fastened herself to the mast. Drenched with rain and chilled to the bone, she was rescued the next morning by a now sober crew. Ezechiel Solomon was able to get one horse to the Island but was unable to have anyone bring it the rest of the way to Penetanguishene. The horse lived and died on Fitzwilliam's Island, but its memory lives on as many people called it Horse Island.

In the spring of 1831, a small detachment of soldiers marched from Fort York to the landing at Newmarket, which was composed of one store and a few buildings. From there they went by

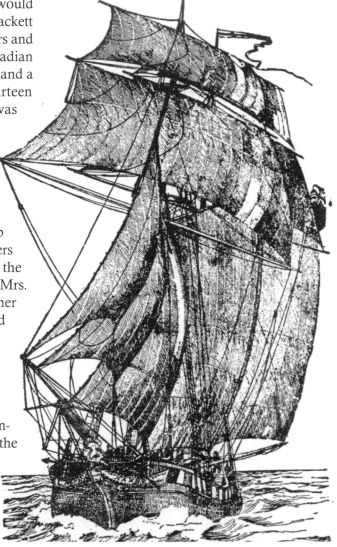

The brig "Wellington" transported personnel from the British post on Drummond Island to Penetanguishene in November, 1828. The schooner "Hackett" with her drunken crew would not be so lucky during the same assignment and voyage.

boat to Barrie, then marched the old military trail towards Penetanguishene. Just north of what is now Elmvale, while crossing through marshy land, one of the soldiers took sick and dropped out of line. His brother, who was also in the small detachment, was allowed to drop back to see what was wrong, and stay with him.

God alone knows the anguish they suffered during that fateful night, harassed as they must have been by mosquitoes, black flies and other insects. The following morning, when they had not yet arrived, a search party was sent out to look for them and found them huddled together, but dead, with no indication of the cause of death.

At the Establishments, across from Magazine Island, lie three graves. One is of a little girl who was much beloved by the garrison and the other two are those of the McGarraty Brothers.

As is evident in these graves and the establishment of the Anglican Garrison Church, Saint James-on-the-Lines, the new residents of Penetanguishene needed spiritual guidance and salvation. But what of the many Catholics who relocated here? Would their needs be met?

Graves at the Establishments in Penetanguishene attest to the fact that life at the military outpost in the 1800's was not without its pitfalls and dangers.
Photo - Midland Free Press

Father John Patrick Kennedy,
5th Pastor of St. Anne's Parish 1860-1873

3

The New Missions

Around 1825, two men entered the picture as the first Catholic lay missionaries of this new era. The first was a good, educated man named Dédin Révol, who moved from Drummond Island. His first converts, Frenchmen, voyageurs and natives seemed almost no more eager to do so then the first Huron. He would round up as many as possible from these three classes of society and teach them Catholicism. After coming to Penetanguishene, he continued this work with varying degrees of success. Finally, determining that the local Catholics deserved better, he returned to Quebec.

At that time, Penetanguishene was in the jurisdiction of Bishop Macdonnell of Kingston and Révol paid him a visit while en route. Although his appeal to the Bishop for a priest for Penetanguishene was not heard immediately, he did promise him help. Révol appar-

ently asked Bishop Lartigues of Montreal for assistance as well. Though not in his jurisdiction, Bishop Lartigues promised to help the hundred odd Catholic families here if he could.

Next came a Scotsman and fur trader from Drummond Island named George Gordon, who had married the daughter of Agnes Landry, a widow of French and Ojibway extraction. He set up his fur trade business to the east of the Establishments which would be named Gordon Point, Military Point, then Reformatory Point and more recently, Ontario Hospital Point. Here, the Metis and landed immigrants built wigwams and shelters covered with cedar bark and awaited the government to give them land. Homesteads were given in twenty or forty acre lots. At the end of the bay where the village would eventually take hold, a few Indian huts were interspersed in a swampy land covered with cedar and poplar down by the water's edge.

George Gordon continued as a fur trader but in his spare time, he practised his Catholic faith and taught it to others. He built the first house in Penetanguishene, which still stands on Water Street and was blessed by every visiting bishop and priest. In 1831, Penetanguishene was already a thriving little village. In 1831, a Father Collins visited Penetanguishene to give the people a few

days of retreat. The following year another priest, Father Bennett remained for a few weeks with George Gordon on Water Street.

In February of 1832, the Catholics of Penetanguishene rejoiced with the visit of Bishop Macdonnell of Kingston accompanied by a Père Crevier. Mass was celebrated in Mr. Gordon's house and the sacraments received by all who attended. Catholic instruction was given, children of various ages baptized and marriages already entered

Bishop Alexander Macdonnell. The visit of Bishop Macdonnell from Kingston, in February of 1832, prompted the Catholics of Penetanguishene to build their first church.

Fur trader and lay missionary George Gordon built the first house in Penetanguishene at 12 Water St. in 1828. Still standing today, his home substituted as a church and rectory for visiting missionary priests and bishops until 1832 when the first log church was built.

into were given the official blessing of the Church. In fact, seven couples completely renewed their vows in front of the bishop and some couples hastened their wedding day in order to have the bishop perform an official ceremony. It should be noted that, in these times, vows of marriage exchanged without the presence of a clergyman were deemed legal, provided there were two witnesses.

After the departure of Bishop Macdonnell, Révol organized the men and soon had the first church under construction. Michael Labatt who helped in building the

In 1832, the first church was built in the parish under the direction of Dédin Révol and George Gordon. Dedicated to St. Anne, the little log church was a powerful testament to the faithful for 29 yrs.

St. Anne's first bell. The first bell to hang from St. Anne's was dated 1799. It came from either the American warship "Tigress" or "Scorpion" when those ships were placed "in ordinary" and stripped of armaments. Seventeen inches height, it weighs 80 lbs. *Photo by Yvon Gagné*

church described this small structure as a log building 21 feet by 32 feet. The cedar logs were placed upright with tennons fitted into the grooves, which were considered an improvement on the overlapping corners of the ordinary log building. There were four windows on each side, two at the entrance on either side of the door. On the top was placed a large cross with the chimney behind it. Beside the door, two logs formed an L-shaped rack from which hung the bell. This bell was used not only to call the people to worship but for fire alarms, for special meetings and other emergencies.

Mr. George Tessier, who died in 1944, related that when his father and his party arrived from Batiscan, Quebec, the bell was rung and the villagers rushed to welcome them. This bell, it is worthy to note, was taken from one of the American ships of war, either the "Tigress" or the "Scorpion" when they were stripped of armaments and placed in ordinary. The bell was then given by the military to the Catholic priest who was the Chaplain at the fort. It stands 17 inches high, is 14 inches in diameter and weighs 80 pounds. It bears in relief, on its side, the date of its birth, "1798".

This log church was built on land donated by Pierre Giroux. It was situated where the present Municipal Offices are located on Robert Street. For the twenty-nine years of its existence, the little log church was a powerful witness to the spirit of faith of the Parish dedicated to St. Anne, the mother of the Virgin Mary.

In September of 1833, Bishop René Gaulin, Co-adjutor of Bishop Macdonnell, made his first visit to Penetanguishene. The First Book of Records showing thirty-one baptisms of children aged between eight days and four years, was commenced by Bishop Gaulin, during that visit.

The first resident priest was a Father Dempsey, who came originally from Glengarry, Scotland. At last the hopes of the people were fulfilled and their prayers answered. However, it appeared that Father Dempsey had begged his Bishop not to be sent to do missionary work due to ill health, a request that fell on deaf ears. Apparently, Father Dempsey's last words to the Bishop were:

"Remember my Lord, now that you are forcing me out on the mission, that I will lay my death at your door."

His words were indeed prophetic, for after three months, Father Dempsey was seized with sudden illness at the Bergen farm near Crown Hill, about six miles north of Barrie. Medical aid was sent from his parish and the priest made as comfortable as possible, but it was to no avail. He died at 5:00

a.m. on November 12th, 1833. His parishioners, led by George Gordon, travelled to the farm and brought his remains here for burial.

Between 1835 and 1873, Penetanguishene was the point of departure for other missionary priests who worked in Simcoe County and the surrounding counties. In all seasons of the year, the records clearly show their zeal in every corner of their parish, which in and of itself, was large enough to make a small diocese. From Manitoulin Island along the East Coast of Georgian Bay to Port Severn, from Orillia through to Barrie, through Owen Sound along the shoreline to Waubaushene, we still see steady traces of their early labours. In summertime, their mode of travel was by boat or canoe where water separated them from their destination or by horse and buggy where roads had been constructed. In springtime, before the break-up, walking or going on horseback was the only possible way to reach souls in need. From December until March horse-drawn sleighs or cutters formed the most convenient method of travel.

Père J. Baptiste Proulx came from Kingston to Penetanguishene in the fall of 1835, having received his commission from Bishop Gaulin on October 27th of that year. On November 10th, his first entry in the Baptismal Register was made when he baptized Sally Ann and Rosalee Preston. Shortly after his arrival, the priest's residence was constructed on lots purchased by Père Proulx.

By July 1st, 1836, Père had baptized about one hundred and twenty-five people, the majority of them being natives. His first marriage, and the first marriage on record in the Parish, was between Paul Chagaichi and Marie Essena. From Sault Ste. Marie to Beausoleil Island, (now Georgian Bay Islands National Park), Père Proulx made a study of the spiritual needs of the native people. His desire to devote himself exclusively to the Indians meant that another priest was needed to reside in Penetanguishene. During this time, Père Proulx and the Jesuits continued to come to Penetanguishene to attend to the Indians of the village and its neighbourhood. Penetanguishene was also visited by the missionary priests Pères Durauquet, Frémiot, Point, Hanipaux, Férard, and Nadeau. Père Proulx was instrumental in obtaining Manitoulin Island as a reserve and attended to them alone for eight years until he obtained the help of the Jesuit Fathers. Père Proulx was then appointed to Oshawa, and later to Toronto.

Père Charest succeeded Père Proulx in 1837 and remained until the time of the great influx of immigrants in 1854. The district under his charge was immense. It extended to the Narrows in the south-east

and to Owen Sound in the south-west which included Collingwood, Barrie, Orillia, Flos, Medonte, Coldwater and Lafontaine. In reading the Parish Records, you follow Père Charest today in Penetanguishene, tomorrow in Coldwater, the next day at the Narrows.

The many French Canadians who came to Penetanguishene and Tiny Township settled as well in Lafontaine, or Ste. Croix as it was known then. These first settlers came from the birthplace of Père Charest; Batiscan and Ste. Anne-de-la-Parade. Other immigrations occurred between 1841 and 1924 and originated from the Quebec areas of Batiscan, Ste. Anne-de-la-Parade, Joliette, St. Anicet, Hutington County and St. Polycarpe in the County of Soulanges, with a sprinkling from the Gaspé.

On the departure of Père Charest, Père Frémiot remained in charge from March to May, 1854. Then Père Claude Ternet was appointed Pastor of Penetanguishene on June 10th, 1854. In the meantime, the mission was divided and Père Ternet's ministrations were confined to the Townships of Tiny and Tay, and parts of Flos and Medonte with churches at Penetanguishene and Ste. Croix (now Lafontaine).

As Père Ternet who was from France, did not speak English, the neighbouring priests used to visit Penetanguishene to attend to those who spoke that language only. Thus we see Fathers Flannery, Synnott, Hobin, Vincent, Mahoney, and Walsh paying visits to Penetanguishene and her missions. The first church in present day Lafontaine, Église Ste. Croix, was built in 1856 and blessed in December of the same year by Père Ternet. The present church was built in 1876 by Père Michel.

On Père Ternet's departure in 1857, a Père Jamot, then in Barrie, seemed to have been in charge of the mission of Penetanguishene until a Père Lebaudy came in October 1857 and remained for three years.

Father J. P. Kennedy arrived in the summer of 1860, to take charge of St. Anne's Parish, its several missions and to be chaplain of the Provincial Boys' Reformatory established on the old military grounds. In 1861, Père Gibra was appointed to take charge of the now separate Parish of Ste. Croix in Lafontaine.

In 1861, a new church was built in Penetanguishene. No doubt it was with sentiments of nostalgia mixed with joy and pride that the parishioners passed by the old log church to enter the newly constructed frame building. The summer months of that year found Father Kennedy with many of his parishioners hurriedly making the new church ready. It was finished and blessed on October 2nd, before the snow came. Ordinary windows now became windows with colored glass, and the church's bell summoned the faithful to mass from a real belfry. Due to the ever-present threat of fire, large barrels of water were placed strategically throughout the new church. In winter, the

The 2nd St. Anne's Church. Built in 1861 by Father John Patrick Kennedy, it replaced the log church and housed a real belfry, stained glass windows and was covered with wood siding. It gave way to services in the basement of the present but unfinished stone church in December, 1890.

26

A Boys' Reformatory was constructed on crown lands overlooking the old Establishments. This picture, taken in the 1890's, shows the boys lined up in front of the large center Reformatory building.

church was heated by the large box stove that had at one time been used to heat the old military barracks.

The town in those days had a night watchman, who was ever on the alert for fire, especially watching the church. The church was where the pails and ladders were kept at the ready. The youths in the town wanted to play a trick on the watchman, who was of Irish descent, so they ran to inform him that some Orangemen had been seen at the church. One of them then rang the bell, which sent the watchman running, to climb the belfry to look for the trouble. The youths pulled the ladder from the roof, leaving the irate watchman screaming at them.

Reverend Father Kennedy was very busy during the remaining years of his life. At Waubaushene, Port Severn, Sturgeon Bay, Victo-ria Harbour and Midland, mill towns sprang up and development began. Evidence of his self-sacrifice during these years between 1860 and 1873 is given in the manner in which he died. On June 25th, 1873, he was with his boys from the Reformatory on an excursion by boat as they steamed back from Mundy's Bay (Midland). Around noon, one of the young lads fell overboard into the chilly waters of Georgian Bay. Moving from the bow of the boat, Father Kennedy quickly jumped in after him when the drowning, struggling boy surfaced. Unintentionally, the struggling boy dragged Father Kennedy under the surface with him and both were drowned.

Thirty-six years after leaving St. Anne's, Père Proulx, her first regular Pastor, was sent to fill in until the arrival of a new pastor in 1873.

Père Théophile Francis Laboureau.
6th Pastor of St Anne's Parish 1873- 1906

4

Arrival of God's Builder

Little did anyone in the town and parish know that on September 23rd, 1873, the arrival of a short, bearded priest sent by Archbishop J.J. Lynch would irrevocably change their history and the surrounding countryside with it. Théophile Francis Laboureau was such a man.

Born in the Diocese of Dijon in the province of Burgundy, France, in the year 1837, he was called to Canada in 1858 by Bishop de Charbonnel. Completing his seminary course in Montreal, he was ordained to the priesthood on June 14th, 1866 and was destined to work in the newly-formed Diocese of Toronto. Under the direction of Right Reverend A. F. Marie de Charbonnel, S.S., D.D., the newly-ordained priest spent the first few years of his ministry in such missions as St. Catherines, Smithville, Thorold, Niagara and Caledon. By 1873, at the age of 36, Archbishop J. J. Lynch commissioned him

to be Pastor of St. Anne's, Penetanguishene and its missions.

At first glance or meeting, he seemed an ordinary man. He was a little below average in height but seemed to be taller because of the long-tailed coat that he always wore. A short, neatly-kept beard covered his chin and a modest mustache spread across his upper lip.

From beneath rather bushy eyebrows, keen eyes portrayed a sensitive, determined and devout soul. People of yesteryear who remembered him recalled his charity, gentleness and determination. He placed sanctity above everything and demanded a deep respect for God and God's work.

Upon his arrival, he found a community composed of many divergent elements. The French people of the parish formed the large majority, their lives influenced by a faith and determination inherited from their pioneering forefathers. On the other hand, the English element was deeply influenced by their militaristic outlook acquired in the British army and association with its base here. A generous sprinkling of Irishmen had found their way to Simcoe County as well and formed the bulwark between these two groups. They were English in language but had the Catholic faith in common with the French. Fringing this assortment of French, English and Irish was the Native component. It is a marvelous tribute to Père Laboureau to be able to say that he integrated these various peoples so as to receive co-operation in his work from them all.

At this time, the lumber industry boomed, which brought an unprecedented prosperity and development to the town. In turn, this brought with it more new settlers until it soon became evident that the church that Father Kennedy had built was inadequate.

In 1875, Père Laboureau oversaw his first building project within the parish when the brick rectory was built. It was a sign of things to come.

In 1879, the Reformatory was detached from the parish and a chaplain was appointed having special charge of the boys in that institution. As well, because of growth that was occurring in the area, Catholics in towns such as Midland had problems meeting. This was evidenced by a situation that occurred to Père Laboureau on one of his visits to the St. Margaret's Mission in Midland that same year. Reeve Lorenzo MacFarlane ran into Père one day on a street in Midland. Word of Midland's Catholics having no place large enough to hold Mass for the growing congregation reached the Reeve's ears so he asked the pastor about wanting to celebrate mass for quite a large group.

"Why yes, Mr. MacFarlane, but unfortunately there is no dwelling house in the town large enough to contain one-tenth of the congregation. We are too poor to build a church but we must have patience."

"Why not use Orange Hall, Père Laboureau?" suggested the resident.

"You are fond of pleasantries, Mr. MacFarlane," replied the good priest.

"I am not joking, Père. I am quite serious. I am local master and I know the brothers would be pleased if you would use it. If you come to my house now, I will get you the key."

The priest took him up on his offer and the following Sunday, in the Orange Hall, Midland Catholics held their first open Mass, officiated by Père Laboureau. It appears that the Reeve had not measured his fellow Orange Lodgemen's enthusiasm correctly. At their next meeting, held the day after the Mass, Lorenzo MacFarlane was apparently voted out of the order, but the precedent had been set and Midland Catholics used the Orange Hall for the next three years.

The old rectory beside the church, built in 1875, served the priests of St. Anne's for over 125 years.

29

The old St. Margaret's Church in Midland, built in 1881 under the pastorship of Père Laboureau, its mission priest.

No doubt this incident ignited the desire of area Catholics to have their own churches in which the visiting missionary priests from Penetanguishene could say Mass. In short order, under the charge of Père Laboureau, who was the missionary pastor of the district, churches were constructed in Midland, Victoria Harbour, Port Severn and Waubaushene, all amazingly built in the same year—1881.

In 1882, the cemetery at St. Anne's Parish extended beside the church along Robert Street where the Town Hall and adjacent buildings now stand. However, the property was too limited and it obstructed the development and growth of the business core. Therefore, it became necessary to relocate the old cemetery to a new, larger location. Père Laboureau proceeded to obtain official permission. It was granted on Tuesday, June 28th, 1881. The land for a new cemetery was purchased from Hermidas Gamelin and Thomas Leduc.

A large crowd came to the new cemetery to be present at the blessing by His Grace, Archbishop J. J. Lynch, assisted by Père Laboureau and a Father McBride. Not long afterwards, the bodies were exhumed from the old cemetery which had served from the time the first church was completed. Apparently, not all bodies were removed at that time, since many skeletons were unearthed when a foundation was dug for the new Dominion Store (now the Pen 2 Theatre beside the Municipal Offices) which was constructed in 1949. These bones had a belated burial in the new cemetery.

A cemetery is a permanent record book of the life of any parish and St. Anne's has many notable persons laid to rest from her early beginnings. Some of them include:

- *Michael Macdonnell*, who died in 1844 at the age of 53 and was a Justice of the Peace, part-time fur trader and former private secretary to Lord Selkirk.

- *John Carty* (McCarthy), who died in 1867, aged 76 and was the stone mason of the Original Officers Quarters at the Establishments,

- *Hypolite Brissette*, who died in 1885 at age 103, and was a man who had led a daring life. He was apparently tattooed from head to foot, crossed the Rocky Mountains and had many thrilling adventures while employed for the Hudson's Bay Company. On one return trip through the prairies, he stopped at the Cree Village of Little Slave

Lake, fell in love with Archange L'Hirondelle, the Chief's daughter and eloped with her one night. Enraged upon this discovery the next morning, the Chief sent a war party after them but with a head start of several hours, Hypolite and his love managed to cross the Ontario border safely. A legend in these parts during his day, he also guided Colonel Henry Woolsey Bayfield between 1820 and 1823, as Bayfield surveyed Georgian Bay, its thirty thousand islands and Lake Huron in an open bateau,

- *Thomas McCrosson,* who died in 1901 at 72 years of age and was a Warden of the Boys Reformatory and a former editor of the Toronto Tribune,

- *Robert J. Parker*, who passed away in 1901, at age 72 and was the first guard of the Boys' Reformatory who escorted the first 40 boys from the Reformatory Prison in Isle-aux- Noix, Quebec in 1860,

- *John Donohue*, who died in 1879 at the age of 75 and owned an old tavern on Garrison Road right behind the old Gendron house on Church St.,

- *Rev. Philibert Rey,* a native of Switzerland, who died in 1887 at age 53 and was the newly installed Catholic Chaplain at the Boys' Reformatory for only a few months before he suddenly passed away,

- *Sergeant James Quigley,* who died in 1886 at the age of 91 and came with the early contingent of soldiers to the establishments,

- *Genevieve Bottineau*, who died in 1904 at the age of 104, came from St. Polycarp, Quebec, had 15 children, and lived through

The reconstructed winter office at the Establishments, of Colonel Henry Woolsey Bayfield, Admiralty Surveyor on the Great Lakes from here between 1820 to 1823.

the reigns of five British Monarchs.

From the Central Mission of Penetanguishene, Père Laboureau's parish was growing. In Penetanguishene, he ministered to 2,030 Catholics, 1,370 in Midland, 260 in Waubaushene, 280 in Port Severn, and 120 in Victoria Harbour. Mass was said every Sunday in Penetanguishene, almost as often in Midland and once a month in the other places. The revenues in the Parish for the year

1883 came to $1,666.00 at a time when the average salary was $15.00 a month.

It is also interesting to note that, at that time, wearing shoes was not the norm for boys. As soon as the snow was gone, bare feet was the going fashion. In fact, the only time shoes were worn was in church. Boys would carry their shoes and socks to church, put them on before entering, and quickly remove them until the next Sunday service. A suit of clothes lasted for years and was handed down from son to son for Sunday services and other special occasions. Waste not, want not!

It became vitally apparent for Père Laboureau to have assistance in his mission. Accordingly, in October 1882, Reverend Michael Jeffcott was sent as the first curate and was succeeded by Father Patrick Whitney in July, 1883. Father Whitney, in turn, was followed by Father Lynett.

In 1883, the Mission of Penetanguishene was again divided: Midland, Waubaushene and Victoria Harbour now constituted a separate parish with Father Lynett as its first resident pastor. Port Severn and Wyevale remained attached to Penetanguishene.

With St. Anne's Parish here continuing to grow larger each day, Père Laboureau had to turn his attentions now to solving his biggest problem: his church here was now simply too small to meet the growing demands of the faith.

He would have to find a solution.

An early drawing of Penetanguishene in 1879. Father Kennedy's church is clearly visible with its steeple rising high above the town's landscape.

An early concept drawing of the planned Canadian National Shrine or Jesuit Memorial Church, to be built in Penetanguishene beginning in 1886.

5

A National Shrine to the Canadian Martyrs

At this point in time, it seemed apparent that the heroism and martyrdom of St. Jean de Brébeuf and his companions had received but scant attention. The Jesuit "Relations", their writings, had been shelved and the story of their lives remained unknown to the world in general. Even locally, their work and deaths were considered like an ancient myth. In light of this, Père Laboureau decided that the brave deeds, self-sacrifice, and the nobility of their lives and death should be resurrected. The memory of the Canadian Martyrs, he thought, should be brought from oblivion and honoured, not only by his own parishioners but by the whole world. In this way, their lives would become a constant source of inspiration to all men.

In his campaign about rendering due homage to the Jesuit Martyrs, this saintly pastor fashioned a two-edged sword. One edge deter-mined to cut down ignorance of their lives and martyrdom. The other edge would be used to replace his small antiquated church but replace it with a fitting memorial—a church that would be a "shrine", erected to commemorate the deeds of Canada's heroic missionaries. It was a bold plan indeed but one which he thought was entirely à propos, since Penetanguishene was the birthplace not only of the Jesuit Missions but of the missions that ensued during the next three hundred years. What was once the birthplace of Catholicism on the farthest Canadian frontier was now again the central Mission of Huronia.

Père Laboureau first obtained permission from Archbishop Lynch to take a leave from his official duties from the parish so he would be able to place all of his vigor into the project at hand. From the begin-ning of his campaign Père Laboureau met great enthusiasm. Archbishop Lynch gave his strong approval, as written in his letter of support for him to take to Europe:

"... I strongly recommend that you receive the blessings and charity of our brothers in the faith, and I ask that they assist you in your beautiful endeavour which you undertake with my blessings and direction ...please note that at the last Council of Baltimore, the advancement towards beatification of Brébeuf's companions who died in the United States has begun, and it is our hope that soon, their names can join with those who suffered the same fate in Canada."

From Archbishop Taschereau of Quebec came this elegant letter of support:

"... I approve wholeheartedly of your plans to build a church in your parish to honour the missionaries who left Quebec in the 16th century to evangelize the natives but who gave of their blood . . . as you depart for Europe to solicit funds and support for your beautiful task, may Saint Raphael guide you in peace, hope and charity."

From retired Arch-Bishop Charbonnel of Toronto, came this letter:

"The notice of your arrival filled me with joy. I was reminded of the words of my successor who spoke to me of your zeal . . . I give you my wholehearted recommendation for your endeavour . . . May God bless your steps, and may you encounter many friends of St. Joseph in honour of the first Canadian Martyrs."

The following was a letter sent to the Lieutenant Governor of Ontario by Mayor Keating of Penetanguishene, dated March 10th, 1881:

A sculpted replica of the Archbishop of Toronto, J.J. Lynch, who encouraged and gave his blessing for Père Laboureau's building plans. *Courtesy Penetanguishene Centennial Museum*

To His Honour
John Beverley Robinson
Lieutenant-Governor of Ontario.

"The Corporation of the Town of Penetanguishene humbly showeth, that the people of Penetanguishene and the French Canadian population of the surrounding district have for years expressed a strong desire, that the Province of Ontario, amidst the scenes of the Huron Missions of 1634, ensure that a fitting monument should be erected to commemorate the events of that time that transpired here and which form in the opinion of all the writers of Canadian and American history, one of the brightest pages in the annals of early Canada. This wish has been echoed from many parts of Canada, and strong expressions of sympathy with the project has been received from many and varied sources, that after due considerations and after consulting the opinions of many well versed in the history of the missions, it has been admitted that, the Bay of Penetanguishene, the birthplace of the Missions, and a site has been selected, from which the towers of the church will form a most noble and striking monument.

"To erect a monument worthy of the men and events is beyond the ability of the residents of the locality altogether, apart from the fact that the recognition of the events to be worthy should be national and not merely local—it will thus be necessary to appeal to the people of the Dominion and possibly to ask the aid of the

Land from which the Missionaries came.

"Before doing so, it is essential to the success of such an appeal should have received the approval of, and have been accepted by the leading men of our Province. We therefore, most earnestly, ask, that your Honour, so well versed as you are known to be in the early history of the county, would grant us the benefit of your great personal influence, and would so endorse and accredit the merits of the undertaking, that in approaching the other Dignitaries of the Dominion, we might be able to show that we have the approval and sympathy of the Lieutenant-Governor of our Province."

W. J. Keating, Mayor of   Penetanguishene
H. Jennings, Clerk.

A reply was received September 9, 1884, from Toronto:

"I cordially agree with the people of Penetanguishene, and the French-Canadian population of the surrounding district, in all they have said in the 'Memorial' through their worthy representative, the Mayor of Penetanguishene, and trust their endeavors, to have erected a fitting monument in honour of the sublime courage and devotion, may meet with success."

John Beverly Robinson,
Lieutenant-Governor of Ontario.

A former Governor-General of Canada, the Marquis of Lorne, also wrote to the town:

"Reverend Laboureau carries with him the best wishes of the municipality where he has lived for twelve years . . . on behalf of many friends across Ontario, we wish him the greatest success in his beautiful endeavour . . ."

W.J. Keating, Mayor of Penetanguishene between 1883 and 1886, was instrumental in galvanizing municipal and townspeople support for Père Laboureau's plans to build a magnificent church.
Courtesy Penetanguishene Centennial Museum.

Marquis of Lorne
1878 - 1883

Support from the Marquis of Lorne, former Governor-General of Canada, certainly helped in Great Britain.

The Lieutenant-Governor of Quebec, Théodore Robitaille, wrote to voice his strong support as well on September 24th of the same year. On October 4th, 1884, a letter arrived from the Office of the Governor General of Canada, Lord Landsdowne, and with it a cheque for fifty dollars.

Lord Landsdowne, Governor General of Canada at the time, was instrumental with his moral and financial support.

Lord Landsdowne 1883 - 1888

Père Laboureau's plans were kicking into high gear. After receiving permission from the Archbishop and the endorsement of the parish, Père Laboureau put into place his ambitious plan of erecting a suitable monument to the Martyrs here in Penetanguishene. He made extensive studies of the Missionaries and gave lectures in different parts of the country and the United States. Most of all, he truly rallied the local citizens and the population of the town and area behind his cause as evidenced by a gathering held in his honour in Council Chambers on the eve before his departure on January 29th, 1886. Mayor Keating spoke on behalf of council and its citizens,

"Learning that you are about to leave town for a few months . . . to Europe . . . on matters connected with the Memorial (church) . . . the Council of Penetanguishene desires to embrace the opportunity of wishing you a happy and prosperous trip and a safe return. The national character of the great work you have undertaken makes it worthy of the sympathy of all Canadians irrespective of creed . . . you have shown yourself imbued with fortitude and earnestness that make you worthy to take charge of the mission founded by these gallant men . . . We wish you God- speed in your mission and a safe and speedy return to your adopted home."

On his departure by train and then by ship, he first journeyed to England armed with a letter from Prime Minister, Sir John A. MacDonald, which opened many doors through our Ambassador to Great Britain, Sir Charles Tupper.

He was favorably received in Great Britain by The Marquis of Lorne, a former Governor General of Canada, and his wife, the Princess Louise, a daughter of Queen Victoria. Their subscriptions along with that of Cardinal Manning was a good start to his trip.

After an absence of more than a quarter of a century, Père Laboureau returned to France, the country of his birth. At Dijon, he had a double mission—first, to appeal for assistance, secondly, to select a style of architecture for the proposed monument.

A letter of support from Prime Minister Sir John A. MacDonald helped give Père Laboureau's appeals for financial assistance at home and abroad instant credibility.

He received substantial support as evidenced by excerpts of this letter from Hector Fabré, Canadian High Commissioner to Paris:

"... I am happy to support your effort which has received such high regard. Your efforts shall be rewarded I'm sure by all of France, as it has been by all Canadians ... I am convinced that you will find as much support in France as you have in Canada, and that soon you will see rise this monument to honour the memory of Brébeuf, Lalement and their companions."

Encouragement poured in from many statesmen in France interested in the Martyred Missionaries, namely the Archbishop of Rouen and the Bishops of Normandy, (the birthplace of Père de Brébeuf), L. P. Morton then U. S. Ambassador to France, and Members of the French Academy, Senators and others.

While Père Laboureau was in France, he selected the style of architecture; the late Romanesque. This style, used for many basilicas built in Europe between A.D. 800-1270, re-emerged architecturally in the 19th century. This style was characterized by rounded arches, clearly articulated ground plans and elevations and had both barrel and rib vaults. Since his project was to be a tribute to France of sorts, Père Laboureau had a French architect from Normandy draw up rough plans which would be representative of the ecclesiastical architecture of the native province of the Martyrs.

At home, his project was gaining steam. He received the blessing and financial support of many eminent persons throughout the Dominion which included the Bishops of Quebec, the Bishops of Ontario, Sir Charles Tupper, Sir Hector Langevin, Sir Wilfrid Laurier, Edward Blake and other Members of Parliament, W. Meredith and Members of the Provincial Legislature, the Mayor of Quebec, the Mayor of Montreal, Hon P. J. Chauveau, L'abbé Verreau of Montreal, Fr. J. C. Taché of Ottawa, and a Dr. Scadding of Toronto.

It is impressive to note that Père Laboureau, at the end of the day, could proclaim that he received assistance and funds to build this Martyrs' Shrine, here in Penetanguishene, from various people and the governments of Canada, France, Great Britain, Ireland and the United States. His efforts had not been in vain.

Upon his return to Canada, Père Laboureau had construction plans drawn up by renowned Architect, Thomas Kennedy. The church was to be constructed of "rough or rock-faced local stone" and the trimmings, moldings, carvings in Credit Valley Stone and Nottawasaga Sandstone. The two transepts on the side of the church were to be used as Chapels and contain the commemorative monuments. These would be adorned with large round- headed windows.

Kennedy tried to make the Shrine less massive in appearance than the true Romanesque style usually called for. To do this, he indented the front entrance wall of the church, in from the large outer columns giving a less weighted appearance.

Sir Charles Tupper, Canadian Ambassador to Great Britain, gave his full moral and financial support towards the construction of Père Laboureau's Shrine in Penetanguishene

The Church Building Committee formed in April, 1886 was composed of the following: Honourary President, Archbishop Lynch of Toronto, President—Mayor W. J. Keating, Secretary-Treasurer—Reverend T. F. Laboureau, Messrs. H. Thompson, P. H. Spohn, M.D., Jos. Cloutier, James Wynne, A. Charlebois, M. J. Mundy and P. Payette. The Penetanguishene branch of the Imperial Bank of Toronto were the bankers.

Dr. Phillip Spohn, the first Reeve of the Village of Penetanguishene, and her first doctor, was a key member of the Church Building Committee.

The site to build the Shrine was chosen by the Memorial Church Committee and purchased. Situated in the most prominent position on a hill at the center of town, it was expected to be quite a sight from the water. Its position in the town was not un-

like many large European Romanesque churches and cathedrals where they were sturdily and intentionally designed to dominate the local population and provide them with a fortress in times of need. As funds poured in and plans fell into place, the much-anticipated construction of the Shrine was set to begin.

Word had traveled far and wide as witnessed by the thousands who poured into town for the official laying of the cornerstone. On Saturday, September 4th, at one o'clock, the Boys' Reformatory Band, under the direction of a Mr. Frederick, played at the Penetanguishene train station as the train of honour arrived. In it were John Beverley Robinson, Lieutenant-Governor of Ontario; Archbishop Lynch; Monsignor O'Brien, the papal representative; the Very Reverend

Dean Harris, the Vicar-General of the Diocese of Peterborough and a noted author; and a Father McBride of Toronto. The party was met by Père Laboureau, Mayor Keating, Members of Council, and a huge crowd. Archbishop Lynch was hosted by Père Laboureau at the Rectory, whereas Mayor Keating entertained the rest of the party for the duration of the weekend at his residence, so as to free up Père Laboureau to make the last minute preparations.

Sunday, September 5th, 1886, was a beautiful but hot day, as two trainloads from Barrie brought almost a thousand pilgrims, as did full steamships from around the Georgian Bay. The "Maxwell" came loaded from Parry Sound, the "Telegram" from Collingwood, the "Chicoutimi" from Waubaushene and Port Severn, the

The train station, located by the town docks, was the lifeblood of the town to the outside world. In the town's heyday the station welcomed four trains a day loaded with goods, merchandise and people.

"Cherokee" from Victoria Harbour and the "Tender" from the Musquash. In the air was great anticipation and excitement, as all the priests of the area as well as a crowd of over five thousand swelled around the church construction site. At noon, Archbishop Lynch presided at a Low Mass in the old church.

A first bell rang at one-thirty and again at two o'clock as the official procession formed. A boy, bearing a crucifix, headed a long line of children, followed by a children's choir. They then were followed by all the area priests in their robes, Monsignor O'Brien in his purple robes, the Archbishop in full robes and Mitre, the Lieutenant-Governor and invited guests. They all made their way accompanied by an honour guard headed by a Captain Landrigan, to a platform with covered canopy at the site of the new Shrine.

 Arriving at the place where the "Cornerstone" was to be laid, Archbishop Lynch went first to a cross, placed where the Altar was to be erected. After the singing of a hymn, which was accompanied on the organ played by Mrs. McCrosson, he then returned to bless the "Cornerstone" of the new Church, invoking God's blessing on all who might help the new building. The Litanies were then said, followed by an antiphon and another hymn.

Using a silver trowel, the Archbishop, with the help of stonemasons, laid the stone in its place and sprinkled it with Holy Water in the Name of the Father and of the Son and of the Holy Ghost. A Latin document from the Archbishop as well as copies of "The Mail", "The Globe", "The World News", "The Penetanguishene Herald" and other publications, along with some coins, were placed in the cornerstone and sealed.

The huge foundation was then sprinkled with Holy Water while another antiphon was said. Coming back to the corner stone, he recited the last prayer, asking that the work, which was to begin for the glory of God, might be accomplished by His gracious assistance. A collection amounting to $500.00 was then taken and placed on the cornerstone. Then Archbishop Lynch addressed the throng:

"We have placed this cornerstone in the church about to be erected . . . it is to be under the invocation of St. Joseph and St. Anne, the mother of the Blessed Virgin, that this parish has been so long conducted and it will be a monument to the heroism of those priests who gave up their lives here for the faith and were put to death in this parish . . . I trust that good Pastor Laboureau will see this church completed . . . and that by the mercy of God, I may be spared to consecrate it at the opening . . . "

The Lieutenant-Governor spoke next and talked about how impressed he was that the support and efforts to build the church were not confined by any religious, sectional or political feelings. Thunderous applause echoed across the countryside when he said that he noticed "that Catholics and Protestants were assisting in getting up the memorial."

This corner stone was laid above ground level at the Southwest corner of the church and can be seen today at the back corner near the new rectory. *Drawing by Del Taylor.*

The Sermon was then preached by the Very Reverend Father Dean Harris of Peterborough, a noted author who wrote several valuable books on the early history of the Church in Canada. The following are excerpts of his sermon:

"Each nation, sometimes each province and city have had their special Apostles—Rome and Alexandria, Gaul and Spain, Germany, Britain or the Green Isle each claim their own Apostle regardless of whether he be a native son or more generally their fellowman who, impelled by the charity of Christ, came to bring them the message of salvation.

"Our own country also has not been without her Apostles that witness unto Christ even to the shedding of their blood . . .

"It was in the village of Atouacha, on the shore of what is now Penetanguishene Bay. There, it was that they (Brébeuf and companions) chose to establish their residence and erect with the help of the Indians their first mission house and chapel, and commence the work of the mission. At every opportunity they assembled the children of the village at their house teaching them the Pater Noster, the Sign of the Cross and to chant some prayers and hymns. At times the elders of the tribe, the keepers of its ancient traditions, were induced to assemble at the house of the missionaries who explained to them the principal points of doctrine and invited them to a discussion of it. They were not satisfied to work in one village singly or in pairs, the

Jesuits journeyed in the depths of winter from village to village, ministering to the sick, baptizing the children in danger of death, seeking to commend their religion by their efforts to relieve bodily distress . . . But still nothing could daunt them…

"In spite of the medicine men and the sorcerers, the Jesuits gradually gained the goodwill and confidence of the Huron population. Their patience, their kindness, their courage, their manifest disinterestedness, the innocence of their lives, the toil which even in the fervor of zeal never failed them, gradually won the hearts of these wayward savages. The chiefs of distant villages came to urge that they would make their abode with them. Though the results of the Missions had been very small, the priests toiled on more courageously, hoping that an abundant harvest of souls would soon reward their labours. The grace of God and the sacrifices of the Missionaries softened the hearts of the Huron and gradually they accepted the Faith, its practices and the moral precepts of Christianity . . .

" A Canadian writer, not a Catholic, sums up in the following noble words the work of the Missionaries which he well may call blessed 'He who reads the story of the self-denying lives and heroic deaths of these Jesuits, although of an alien race and different belief, will surely feel a throb of sympathy for their sufferings and of exaltation in their lofty courage and unfaltering faith,

An early portrait of the North American Martyrs.

the Missionaries perished in their victory and were buried in their triumph".

The Dean went on at length in describing the deaths of Brébeuf and Lalement and concluded his remarks with the following:

" . . . it was proposed to erect at Penetanguishene, the birthplace of the Huron Mission, the centre of the traditions of the past and of the scenes of their apostolic labours and heroic deaths, a Memorial Church as a fitting monument to those brave, holy and noble men— to recall and perpetuate their memory and the history of the Mission. The project received the sanction and encouragement of the Bishops of both provinces, Ontario and Quebec and of other parts of the world and also of men prominent in the ecclesiastical, political, literary and social world."

Then Père Laboureau rose to speak:

"Having charge of the Penetanguishene Mission, the honour and the burden of the work naturally fell on my shoulders. The work was commenced a few years ago and is progressing slowly towards completion. It has always been considered that the nature of the undertaking and the object to be commemorated should enlist the generous sympathy of all, especially the people of Canada and prompt them to help and share in the erection and completion of this memorial. It has been brought to the consideration of the Reverend Jesuit Fathers, to whom I wish to express my most sincere thanks for the encouragement I have received from them and by whose kind permission

This revealing picture of the Main St. taken circa 1898, shows very clearly the town in its infancy. Note the still unfinished church in the top right.

I now make this appeal for the building of our Memorial Church."

Archbishop Lynch then pronounced a final blessing and the festivities concluded.

For the first three years, the stonework on this huge church progressed slowly but steadily. By June of 1889, there were just a few feet of the upper walls to lay and work progressed only as Père Laboureau could collect enough funds to resume work. Still, by December 1890, four years after the digging of the huge foundation and the blessing of the cornerstone, the main section of his beloved new church was roofed, much

to his relief. He prepared the basement, and that Christmas, the first service was held there.

In retrospect, it must have been a daunting task for the small parish to have even attained this stage. Already, it was a gigantic structure with its three-foot-thick walls set 50 feet apart that rose almost a hundred feet into the air from the base of the foundation. The outside of the large, imposing columns that graced each side of the front of the church was almost a hundred feet apart. It was truly magnificent! It dwarfed the small church that Father Kennedy had built.

Père Laboureau's zest for building funds was completely unselfish, as he not only made a vow of poverty but, steadfastly kept it in every detail. *"He was fortunate on many an occasion to be wearing a long-tailed coat,"* wrote one of his fellow priests, *"because he was always giving away not only the shirt off his back, but sometimes his trousers. Once he had to go to bed in order to have his only remaining pair of trousers repaired."* Such was the life and times of Père Theophile Francis Laboureau.

The building of this huge shrine in Penetanguishene was without doubt the story of the life of Père Laboureau. It was his mission and he attacked the task with a zeal and dedication of ten men. Despite the fact that this tenure would require of him to ask constantly for money from whomever he met to help finish his dream, still in his heart he was a priest of the same missionary mould as the Jesuits whom he wished to honour. Those who remembered him recalled his devotion to minister to his flock first and foremost.

"One night in winter," recalled one parishioner of his day, *"he made a long cold journey by cutter to Port Severn to attend a sick parishioner. On his return he was asked by his* curate: 'How was the patient, Father? She must have been very sick to have you travel thirty miles on a night like this?' *In his charitable way, Father replied with the light and joy of*

This beautiful painting done by artist Del Taylor envisions the scene that driver Eddie Dubeau recalled that stormy night when he gazed through the driving snow back at a praying Père Laboureau.

sincerity in his eyes, 'Thank God, she was able to meet me at the door'."

"One night in late February" recalled another, *"while on the way to a sick call somewhere on the North Shore, Father's horse fell through the ice. The wicked snow swept south from Manitoulin Island and the open Bay. It was decided that Father Laboureau remain with the cutter and Eddie Dubeau, the driver, should go for help. Mr. Dubeau to his dying day remembered the picture Father Laboureau presented that evening. Looking back over his shoulder as he made for shore and help, he could see the kneeling figure of Father Laboureau, his Breviary in one hand and a candle in the other. The amazing part of it all was that, in spite of the whirling wind, the candle kept on burning."*

Still, his Church was his reason for existing. It appeared that there was considerable pressure from the Archdiocese to open the church as soon as possible, as evidenced by this article published in October of 1892:

"The . . . (completion of the church to the point of usage), has not been realized. The Memorial Church still stands unfinished. Truly by the contributions of the people, the aid of kind friends interested in the work, and unfortunately, the means of too heavy a loan . . .

"It is the wish of His Grace, the Archbishop of Toronto, to have the church completed and ready for opening in May, 1894. In the meantime, Père Laboureau will devote himself to the arduous work of collecting funds. Encouraged by his Archbishop, who commends him to the kindness of friends of the work, he hopes to see his work completed, and the Memorial Church of the Missionary Martyrs dedicated to the worship of God and opened to the public at the time mentioned."

Despite his best efforts, it did not happen. Due to its massive size and cost, the Shrine required sixteen long years to be completed. It was a slow and labourious process. Great detail and care were taken in the colour schemes of stone used for certain sections. The lime used in the mortar was made at Pinery Point by Narcisse Dubeau, and Joseph Dubeau supervised the stone work.

This spectacular photo shows a temporary, wooden roof over the unfinished right tower of the church as it looked in 1898, 12 years after the laying of the cornerstone.

This photo of one of St. Anne's original stonemasons, Henry Zoschke and his wife Augusta, taken in front of the stone home he constructed in then Tay Township, behind Fuller Avenue.

The foundation was built of hand-cut stone from Quarry Island, and the church's walls composed of rock-faced granite and fieldstone, trimmed with Credit Valley stone and white Nottawasaga Sandstone.

Romanesque types of architecture frequently used roughly finished stone, so that the texture and richness of the stone would be enhanced by the shadows caused by the sun. Père Laboureau's church would be a classic example of this upon completion.

In 1898, the huge left front column was still not finished with there being about ten feet of stone at the top to lay, its opening covered by a large tarp. But finally, the stonework, the bulk of this massive construction project, was complete. Père Laboureau then turned his attention to the inside. The Beck Lumber Company, the McGibbon Company and the Victoria Harbour Lumber Company all donated a railcar full of lath to plaster the walls.

Finally, the church was finished in the Fall of 1902. Amazingly, the cost of this massive 16-year project came in at $50,000.00 for just the basic church structure. By comparison, the Église Ste. Croix in Lafontaine was built in 1877 for the then huge sum of $18,000.00, St Patrick's Church in Perkinsfield was built and finished for $4,000.00 in 1884, and in 1914 a completed St. Margaret's in Midland was built for $26,588.00. Keep in mind that in 1900 a loaf of bread cost 2¢, a gallon of milk 20¢, and one could buy a reasonable new home for $300.00.

Now, with the church for all intent and purposes finished, the pressure to officially open it grew, as witnessed by these comments read by a representative of the congregation at the official dedication and opening which finally took place on December 11th, 1902:

"Here we must advert to the unfinished state of the church as is, at present, observable and to explain that it was in contemplation not to have the dedication services performed until next year. But,

in deference to the expressed wish of his Grace, we endeavoured to do within one month the work of six . . . The expenditure in this completion also had to be commensurately crowded into the short period. The latter, necessarily caused a deficit in the funds immediately on hand, but we are hopeful, depending on the continued generosity and goodwill of the congregation, and the expected goodwill and generous assistance of our friends at home and abroad, that the deficit in question will be covered before the coming summer."

Bishop McEvay of London was present at the opening of the church on December 11th, 1902. As Archbishop of Toronto, he would later come to bless and consecrate the bells and the stations of the cross in January, 1909.

This photo shows the wooden stairs at the side of the church before the present side entrance was constructed. Note the separate entrance to the church's basement.

At the liturgical blessing of the new Church of St. Anne, dedicated to the Memory of the Jesuit Martyrs, Most Reverend D. O'Connor, Archbishop of Toronto, and The Most Reverend Charles Gauthier, Archbishop of Kingston, were present and assisted by the Most Reverends Bishop Richard O'Connor of Peterborough and Bishop F. P. McEvay of London. For the opening, Mr. Alphonse Tessier donated the main altar.

At the time of the opening, there were no pews and only some of the windows on the right side of the church were in place.

Still, support continued to come, sometimes from exceedingly high places. Père Laboureau, in May of 1903 sent a receipt to Archbishop O'Connor acknowledging his $500.00 payment, *"with sincere gratitude"*. Then, shortly thereafter, came a donation from very high, namely, the newly appointed young Cardinal, Raphael Merry del Val, the first truly great Vatican Secretary of State, whom many considered a certainty to succeed his beloved friend and mentor, Pope Pius X.

The grounds were soon terraced and the space between the wide front doors and the street were spanned by cement and wooden steps with iron and wooden guard rails. On either side was a six-foot retaining wall for the terrace. It was intended at first to have two side entrances but the one on the right did not materialize since it was not needed.

In November of 1904, the pews were placed and two years later the Sacred Heart Altar was installed. In 1907, the Blessed Virgin's Altar was added. Mr. Tessier presented the pulpit for Easter the following spring.

This early 1908 postcard demonstrated the pride there was in the church despite the fact that its interior was plain except for the pews, altars, confessionals and pulpit.

On October 22nd of the same year, Père Laboureau passed away at the age of 71 and his remains were conveyed here to Penetanguishene. During the funeral ceremonies, Penetanguishene and area paused to honour this amazing man. Main Street, all places of business, the mills and factories were closed. From all walks of life here and from the surrounding countryside, came hundreds, nay thousands, to pay a last token of respect to their old friend who had done missionary work in their midst for 33 years. In his beloved Memorial Church, this National Shrine he had built to honour the Canadian Martyrs, the first Parish of Huronia bade goodbye to its good friend and shepherd.

Bishop John T. Kidd. As Father Kidd, he came as an assistant in 1904 and was in charge of the parish between the resignation of Père Laboureau in 1906 and the arrival of Père Brunet in 1908.

Père Théophile Francis Laboureau 1837 - 1908.

During the latter years, Père Laboureau was assisted by Père Charles Cantillon and Father Grant and later by Father Kidd. A short time after the arrival of Father Kidd in 1904, Père Laboureau was stricken by a paralytic stroke on February 6th. He was incapacitated until May and a Père Minchau was sent to assist. In 1905, Père Phillipe Brunelle was sent as second curate.

Even with this severe handicap, Père Laboureau continued to direct the parish for almost two years. In 1906, he resigned and went to spend the remaining years of his life at Providence House in Toronto. Father J. T. Kidd was left in charge of the parish until the arrival of Père Henri Brunet from the Diocese of Kingston. This was in June of 1908.

Père Henri Brunet.
7th Pastor of St. Anne's 1908-1915

6

Let Us Beautify This House

In the year 1908, a new pastor came to St. Anne's Parish, in the person of Père Henri Brunet. He was to do the very important work of solidifying the foundations so painstakingly laid by his predecessors.

Père Henri Brunet was born in 1879 in France, in the Diocese of Luçon where once the great Richelieu was Bishop. From St. Laurent-sur-Sèvre, the young man went to study in Brittany and also studied a year in Holland. Around the age of eighteen, he was induced to come to Canada and study for the priesthood. After four years of further study in Ottawa, he was ordained on June 1st, 1901. Being only 22 years of age he remained for a year with the Bishop who ordained him. Later, he tells of going from one diocese to another wherever there was need of a French-speaking curate. Archbishop Gauthier of

Kingston used to go on long walks with Père Brunet to learn French from the young priest. Bishop McEvay later took him to London where he remained about two years. Then in 1908, when Bishop McEvay was made Archbishop of Toronto, he knew he would have need of Père Brunet in the northern part of his new diocese in Penetanguishene.

Upon arriving here, Père Brunet was faced with several, immediate, large problems, the most pressing of which was a debt of $16,000.00 on the church. There were no Stations of the Cross, no statues, no ornamentation on the walls and even the bell to call the people to prayer was still the old war bell.

His parishioners also wished to have a memorial of Père Laboureau placed in their church. It was a unanimous decision to erect three bells, one in memory of Père Laboureau, one in memory of Père Brébeuf and one in memory of Père Lalemant. The bells were made in France by the F.& G. Paccard Bell Foundry, the same company that had cast the bells for St. Patrick's Cathedral in New York. The cost of the three bells came to $1,400.00.

On January 10th, 1909, Archbishop McEvay of Toronto presided at the two-fold ceremony of blessing the Statues and consecrating the three memorial bells. High Mass was said and Père LaMarche, Rector of Sacred Heart Church in Toronto, delivered the sermon. The Bishop washed the bells with Holy Water and anointed each with oil in the sign of the Cross. The large bells sat on the floor at the front of the church before the main altar for this ceremony

Following are the inscriptions and names engraved on the bells:

FIRST BELL — 1500 *pounds –key of G*
I praise the true God — I call the people.
I convene the clergy — I bewail the dead.
I dispel the clouds — I grace the festival.
My Name is **THÉOPHILE Pius**
In Memoriam of Théophilus Laboureau
Parish Priest of Penetanguishene, 1873-1906.
I bewail the dead Pastor

SECOND BELL — 800 *pounds* —key of B
In the morning, at noon
and in the evening,
I will ring Thy praises and extol Thy glory.
My Name is **JEAN PATRICK**
In Memory of Jean de Brébeuf, 1649.

THIRD BELL — 475 *pounds* —key of D
I am, and I will ring to the Lord
And you will hear my voice.
My Name is **GABRIEL HENRI**
In Memory of Gabriel Lalemant, 1649.

The Laboureau Bell. Dedicated to the great pastor and builder.

The Brébeuf Bell. Dedicated to the memory of a Saint who walked and lived on the shores of Penetanguishene Bay.

The Lalement Bell. Dedicated to a Martyr who died in this first Parish of Huronia.
Photos by Yvon Gagné.

After the blessings of the bells, the Archbishop blessed and dedicated the fourteen Stations of the Cross which ornamented the pilasters of the church. The beautiful works of statuary were manufactured by the German firm of the Munich Statuary Company of Milwaukee, Wisconsin, as also were the two angels with brass candlesticks on each side of the Main Altar. Other groups of statuary such as the "Dead Saviour", the "Pieta", and the "Holy Family" are the work of the Italian firm: T. Carle, Montreal. The Stations and Statuary with their necessary additions were presented by members and friends of the congregation at a total cost of twelve hundred dollars. The following is the list of the donors:

Stations of the Cross
Mr. and Mrs. Joseph Cloutier; Altar Society; Daniel and Herman Charlebois; Mrs. M. Mundy and children; Mr. and Mrs. F. S. Grist; Michael and C. G. Gendron; Mrs. H. Colombus; Mr. and Mrs. D. A. Lahey; Mr. Ed. Tessier; Mr. Alfred Robitaille; Mr. Napoleon Payette; Florestine Tessier; Mr. and Mrs. James Lavery; Mr. and Mrs. James Wynne.

Sanctuary Railing
Mr. W. Cane of Newmarket

Dead Saviour
Florestine Tessier

Holy Family
G. Bowman, M.D.

Adoring Angels
John J. Hurley

The Memorial Bells
Sir Wilfrid Laurier; Duke of Norfolk; Howard Spohn; Fred Courtemanche; Alfred Thompson.

On Monday, January 11th, the bells tolled for a Requiem Mass for Père Laboureau. On January 12th, the bells were sounded for the wedding of Mr. W. Houlahan and Miss Mary Agnes Columbus.

Later that month, Père Brunet wrote to the Archbishop with descriptions of the two large tablets that were being mounted at the side altars in memory of Pères Brébeuf and Lalement and another to remember Père Laboureau. *"I have also had donated a statue (with bracket) of St. Gabriel, to the memory of Père Gabriel Lalement, at a cost of $100.00 and am awaiting an answer for a St. Jean to match."* At this time he also wrote an addendum, *"I have made arrangements to have the bells raised on the tower under shelter as soon as the weather permits."*

Wilfrid Laurier, one of Canada's Greatest Prime Ministers. Having visited our town, he donated money not only to the original building of the church, but also donated money towards the Memorial Bells.

The bells were placed in the summit of the tower in March of 1909. Along with the new bells, the old bell, which had been in the first two churches, was placed in the tower as well.

The ancient custom of everyone present coming in turn to ring the newly raised bells was followed and for twenty minutes the church bells pealed over the town. A few hours later, they graced the festival at the christening of Anna Leona, daughter of Mr. and Mrs. D. J. Charlebois.

On February 6th, 1910, was the inauguration of the new Pipe Organ. The organ, built by the Matthew's Church Organ Company and placed over the main entrance in the choir loft, was blessed by the Chancellor of the Diocese, Reverend Father Kidd, former parish priest here. Almost eighteen hundred dollars had been collected by means of Garden Parties and One Day's Wages Envelopes.

The organist was Miss Loretta Martin and the choir directress was Mrs. George E. Tessier. The first private service for which the new organ was played was for the marriage of Mr. Octave Montgrain to Miss Louise Gendron. Mr. Philip Montgrain, son of this couple, became an organist for the parish for many years as well.

Père Brunet was a simple, unassuming man, but when needed, his resolve was as strong as iron. For many years, the people on "the other side of the bay - the American side", talked of the houseboat where Père used to gather the young to teach them their

Catechism. He also taught every morning in the basement of the church whether fasting or not. "*It was the only time I could have the children for instruction,*" he often said, "*because we were not allowed to teach religion in the school.*" He always put the spiritual welfare of others ahead of himself and many times he was alone tending to the spiritual needs of his large parish. At that time, there were over 500 families.

In the short space of seven years, Père Brunet finished the interior of the church. By means of a steady campaign of nickels

This photograph was originally dated 1900, but the bells are clearly in the new bell cupola, which was installed in the spring of 1909, and the priest bears a striking resemblance to Père Brunet who orchestrated their ascent. Note the ornate wooden stairs at the front and the lack of a retaining wall down by the street.

and dimes, bazaars, sales, and card-parties, the necessary funds were raised until the church was truly completed.

From the vestibule, three archways opened into the body of the church. Upon entering, your eyes were caught by its utter simplicity and size, a building capable of seating 1,000 worshippers, having inside dimensions of 137 ft. by 45 ft. The main altar, set back in the high-vaulted alcove, formed the sanctuary. On either side of this alcove were the side altars. To the left, on the Gospel side, was that of Mary, Jesus' Mother and on the right, the Epistle side, were the Sacred Heart altar. The transepts or arms of the church, were situated about one third of the way down the body of the church. The one on the Epistle side was used as a Baptistry, and both had confessionals placed against the rear walls. As was customary in churches in Canada, the choir loft was placed over the vestibule.

The murals and stained-glass windows were of exceptional merit. They

49

told in pictures the outstanding events of the life of Christ. The first mural at the front of the church portrayed the Holy Family in their home at Nazareth; the next depicted Jesus surrounded by little children, then an artistic conception of the raising of the daughter of Jairus from the dead by Jesus. First, on the opposite wall nearest the back, was The Last Supper, then the Condemnation of Christ by Pontius Pilate. Lastly, there was pictured Jesus' Ascension into Heaven.

At a height of some fifteen feet up the walls of the church were systematically arranged, apertured windows in groups of three, with a space of about six feet between each group. In the first group of windows, on the left, beginning from back to front was the Annunciation; in the next group it was the Crucifixion. Then, the series was broken by a window dedicated to St. Patrick, and another to St. Anne, Patroness of the parish.

In the rear choir loft, the last window on that side depicted the Resurrection. Other windows showed the Descent of the Holy Ghost, the Sacred Heart of Jesus, the Blessed Sacrament, the Good Shepherd, St. Margaret of Scotland and Saint Gertrude. In the transepts the windows were much larger and pictured "The Assumption" and "St. Patrick".

Beside the main altar were statues of the Patron of our country, St. Joseph and the Patroness of our Parish, St. Anne. At the time of the church's construction, the Canadian Martyrs were themselves not yet declared saints and could not be publicly venerated by public image so statues of their patrons—St. John the Apostle and St. Gabriel the Archangel were installed. These statues were placed on brackets to the left and right of the huge archway that marked the entrance of the sanctuary proper. The only other images were those also situated in the transepts. In the left transept was that of "The Pieta"—Our Blessed Mother holding Jesus' Body in Her Arms after the Crucifixion. In the other alcove was the group of figures representing the Holy Family.

Over the large sanctuary arch, there was a huge mural of the Crucifixion; above the Main Altar, the Martyrdom of

Brébeuf and Lalemant and spread throughout the body of the church, other subjects were depicted to teach the faithful.

Much of what was initially involved in the completion and beautification of the church has remained intact to this day, such as the statuary, and stained glass windows and most of the murals.

At this time, Père Brunet wrote to his Archbishop to indicate that he had paid $200.00 to register the lot at the back of the church for use as a public school. A Public School Board was formed and an agreement between it and the Protestant Separate School Board

This photo shows the interior of the church as it basically appeared from the time of Père Brunet after 1909 until the major renovations done by Monsignor Castex in 1960. *Photo courtesy of Ted Light*

The Beauty of St. Anne's

She has been called: "the Cathedral of the North", "the Canadian National Shrine", "the Jesuit Memorial Church" or more simply "St. Anne's". Many superlatives have been used to describe her exterior and interior beauty down through the years.

Indeed, successive pastors have been inspired by the example set by Père Laboureau through the magnificent church that he built. They, in turn, decorated it to a high standard that he would have been proud of. St. Anne's magnificent statuary, murals, and stained glass windows all evoke very powerful religious symbolism. Described by one visiting artist as, "one giant, beautiful, undiscovered masterpiece", the following colour pages, photographed by renown local photographer Michael Odesse, demonstrate how St. Anne's is clearly one of the most beautiful churches in all of Canada. She is undoubtedly the "Jewel of Georgian Bay".

Père Joseph Lecaron

Père Laboureau's Jesuit Memorial Church - Canadian National Shrine

St. Anne and Mary

The Coronation of Mary in Heaven

The Lamb of God

Stations of the Cross

"The beauty of her stained glass"

A Station
of the Cross

The
Holy
Trinity

Stations
of the Cross

St. Catherine

The Good
Shepherd

St. Charles

Ste Thérèse
de Lisieux

St. Bernadette's vision of
Mary at Lourdes

St. Mark, Evangelist

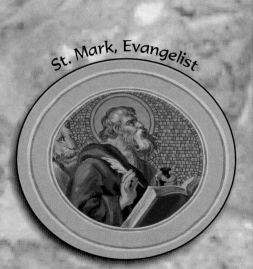

Jesus blessing the children

St. John, Evangelist

Mural of the Pentecost

Mural of the marriage of Mary and Joseph

Main altar of St. Anne's today

St. Matthew, Evangelist

St. Luke, Evangelist

JEAN DE BREBEUF S.J.

GABRIEL LALEMANT S.J.

The Holy
Family in
Nazareth

The
Assumption
of Mary

St. Anne
and Mary

Christ raising Jairus' daughter

Mosaic of
the
Last Supper

St. Margaret of Scotland

St. Charles of Barromeo

The Ascension of Jesus
over the Altar of the Blessed Sacrament

The Canadian Martyrs

"And they will be filled with The Holy Ghost"

St. Joseph and Jesus

VISION OF SACRED HEART

Statue of Blessed Virgin Mary

St. Patrick preaches to the Chiefs of Erin

60

ÉGLISE COMMEMORATIVE DES JESUITES
SANCTUAIRE NATIONAL DU CANADA

THE JESUIT MEMORIAL CHURCH
CANADIAN NATIONAL SHRINE

ERECTED 1886

UNDER THE DISTINGUISHED AUSPICES OF

HIS EMINENCE CARDINAL MERRY DEL VAL
HIS EMINENCE CARDINAL MANNING
HIS EMINENCE CARDINAL TASCHEREAU
HIS EMINENCE CARDINAL GIBBONS
THE ARCHBISHOP OF ROUEN
AND THE BISHOPS OF NORMANDY
HIS GRACE ARCHBISHOP LYNCH OF TORONTO
HIS GRACE THE DUKE OF NORFOLK
EARL-MARSHALL OF THE BRITISH EMPIRE
LE SÉNAT DE LA RÉPUBLIQUE FRANÇAISE
L'ACADEMIE FRANÇAISE
MGR. LE COMTE DE CHARBONEL
HIS EXCELLENCY L. P. MORTON
AMERICAN AMBASSADOR TO FRANCE
HIS EXCELLENCY THE MARQUIS OF LORNE
GOVERNOR-GENERAL OF CANADA
RT. HON. SIR JOHN A. MACDONALD
PRIME MINISTER OF CANADA
RT. HON. SIR CHARLES TUPPER
SECRETARY OF STATE
SIR HECTOR LANGEVIN
HON. EDWARD BLAKE
SIR WILFRID LAURIER
HON. JOHN BEVERLEY ROBINSON
LIEUTENANT-GOVERNOR OF ONTARIO
SIR TH. ROBITAILLE
LIEUTENANT-GOVERNOR OF QUEBEC
THEIR WORSHIPS THE MAYORS OF
MONTREAL, QUEBEC, TORONTO,
FRANCIS PARKMAN
GILMARY SHEA
L'ABBE TH. F. LABOUREAU
THE CITIZENS OF PENETANGUISHENE.

"They built St. Anne's"

"The Pieta"

The Crucifixion   St. Patrick   The Anunciation

Jesus before Pilate

St. Joseph
and Jesus

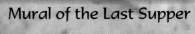

Mural of the Last Supper

St. Anne
and Mary

Large mural of The Resurrection

Her new steeples reach heavenward

reached. As well, at that time, the Altar Society in the parish collected $125.00 for a cork carpet for the main aisle of the church, "*which I fought*" Brunet wrote, and $100.00 for stationary.

In June of 1913, Toronto Archbishop Neil McNeil came to Penetanguishene to give confirmation to 240 children. After arriving by train, he was escorted to the church, where he was addressed by Mayor Louis Gignac.

"*We are proud of our Church, a memorial to our Fathers in the Faith, and we hope to see it free of debt soon. Only yesterday, we heard with pleasure, that new property had been acquired by the parish, for the convents uses, if needed, and we have heard that it is the desire of your Grace, that we should provide for our children, and the future of our Catholic population, by making as far as possible, our school, our own Roman Catholic Separate School, in accord with civil law.*"

In September, 1915, Archbishop McNeil sent Père Brunet to Lafontaine and appointed Père Philippe Brunelle as the new Pastor of St. Anne's.

Born on March 2nd, 1877 in the village of Lafontaine, Philippe was the son of Théophile and Emma (Marchand) Brunelle. Young Brunelle grew up like any other boy of his time, working hard on the farm and building and repairing the equipment. Having received the call of God, he undertook his studies in the town of Trois-Rivières. After completing these, he prepared himself for the Grand Seminary in Quebec and he was ordained by Archbishop O'Connor of Toronto on February 2nd, 1906.

Père Brunelle came to Penetanguishene as assistant to Père Laboureau, from whom it was said that he learned a great deal. Père Brunelle's love of the poor and his willingness to sacrifice his own security for their sake received its greatest impetus at this time. Père Laboureau went to stay in Toronto that autumn of 1906 and Father Kidd remained as administrator until 1908, with Père Brunelle as his assistant. Then, after only two years, Père Brunelle was entrusted with the Parish of Ste. Croix, in his native village of Lafontaine.

Beginning his pastorship here only in 1915, Père Brunelle was assisted by Fathers Doyle, Graff and William Norbert. Père Brunelle carried out his duties through some of the most difficult years that

this young country of Canada and the Penetanguishene area had ever faced. He apparently entered many homes to bring the sad news of the death of a son or father during the First World War. He grew very close to his flock but no doubt the toughest challenge he had to face came during the nightmarish Spanish flu epidemic which swept through the area in 1918.

Early in 1919, with the help of another newly ordained young priest named Père Athol Murray, Père Brunelle showed an abandon that would have ruined a lesser man, as he attended to the sick of three parishes. Father Barceleau of St. Margaret's in Midland, and Père Brunet in Lafontaine, became victims of the dreaded disease and while they hovered between life and death, Père Brunelle strove to give the Sacraments to as many sick and dying as he could. His curate, Father Norbert, died when the epidemic first hit the small town.

Père Philippe Brunelle
8th Pastor of St. Anne's Parish
1915-1938

Under the direction of Père Murray, as many local beds as possible were rounded up, denominations notwithstanding and the Methodist Church was transformed into a makeshift hospital. Even the brass bed of the Methodist prelate was used which prompted one local headline to state, "Chinaman dies in Archbishop's bed."

For two weeks, Père Brunelle drove himself without sleep until his body could stand no more and he succumbed to exhaustion. He was apparently troubled for many years afterward with the thought that so many died without warning, without the sacraments, as he could only physically be in one place at one time. It had been suggested that, in later years when Father Brunelle himself became very ill, that these weeks of physical and mental torment had a delayed effect on his health.

Besides the spiritual welfare of his people, this kindly priest did his utmost to maintain his church and other buildings in good repair. He was responsible for the beautiful pointing which finished the stonework on the church. The sacristy and the roof too demanded much improvement. In 1921, the interior was decorated.

It is a great tribute to Père Brunelle that hundreds came to get his advice and went away with clothing or money to set them up in their work. He bought nets for the fishermen and new suits and dresses for many an aspirant for their First Communion or Confirmation. Children from the Mission of St. David's across the bay were also fed while preparing for these big moments in their lives. It was said that Père Brunelle's many gifts of kindness and charity made many weep or smile with the mere mention of his name.

Under Père Brunelle, advances were made with the local school curricula. Penetanguishene, with its predominantly French-speaking population at the time, were deprived of their right to have their children taught in their native tongue. After almost a half century of contention, Père Brunelle was the driving force that remedied this unacceptable situation. Under the supervision of the Holy Cross Sisters or Soeurs-de-Ste-Croix de St. Laurent, Quebec, the children were able to learn in English and French in the new "bilingual" public school.

From 1919 to 1923, Père Brunelle was assisted by Père Athol Murray, who had organized a hospital during the flu epidemic. The town fathers wanted a celebration to mark the end of the war in Europe and recognizing his organizational skills, asked Père Murray if he would help organize the event.

This old photo of Simcoe St. from in front of the library looking down towards the Thompson Green Block, shows the old Methodist Church on the left, which was a makeshift hospital during the Spanish Flu epidemic of 1919. *Courtesy Penetanguishene Centennial Museum.*

Procuring the permission of Père Brunelle, Père Murray agreed but instead convinced the town to celebrate the tercentenary of the arrival of Champlain and the missionaries to Penetanguishene in 1615. With the war having disrupted plans, which should have occurred in 1915, the town, under Père Murray's leadership, decided to celebrate "Old Home Week" in 1921.

An incomplete letter from the parish, presumably from Père Murray, indicated that he had his sights set on a large, bronze statue of Champlain, cast in England and delivered to Orillia the year before, but not erected. Though it did eventually end up in Orillia's Tudhope Park, the statue, *"distinctly Catholic in tone . . . would have been more appropriate here"*, the letter stated.

Père Murray quickly turned his attention to other matters. Along with his pastor Père Brunelle, and Père Brunet in Lafontaine, Père Murray engineered the Knights of Columbus here and the farmers of Lafontaine, to erect a monument celebrating the first mass in Ontario at the old native village site of Carhagouha. On August 2nd, Archbishop Neil McNeil of Toronto presided over the event that kicked off Penetanguishene's grand historical celebrations. In attendance was Premier Ernest Drury, a former Barrie farmer.

Mobilizing a cast of hundreds on August 3rd, 1921, they re-enacted the landing of Champlain on Penetanguishene Bay, at Huronia Park on Fox St. The ceremony included two giant canoes paddled by neutral Ojibwa Indians. The first canoe carried Iroquois Chief André Staats in full attire, and the five head Sachems of the Iroquois confederates: Mohawk, Oneidas, Onondagas, Cayugas and Senecas. In the second canoe came Huron Grand Chief Ovide Sioui, accompanied by a sub-Chief. They had come all the way from Lorette, Quebec.

Stepping silently together on soil that 300 years before had borne the last blood-filled conflict between the two great Indian nations, the parties moved towards a blood red boulder. A peace pipe was lit and reverently passed from mouth to mouth. As an ancient tomahawk was buried at the foot of the boulder, the Iroquois Staats turned to his Huron counterpart saying, *"Now we go hunt moose!"* Sioui answered *"Together!"* The ceremony marked the first official peace between the Huron and Iroquois nations, sealed by their ancestors, here on Penetanguishene Bay that sun-filled August day. John Milway Filion, the Jesuit Superior General, took his stand with the group at their request to officially witness the final reconciliation. But Père Murray's organizing skills had loftier, more heavenly plans.

This photo of participants was taken after the unveiling of the LeCaron Statue in front of the Memorial Church, during the "Old Home Week" celebrations of 1921. Père Athol Murray, the architect of the celebrations, is at lower left.

In 1920, a young resident named Gérald Lahaie had decided to join the Jesuit order. In so doing, he relinquished the family's fortune which had been promised him by his father D.A. Lahaie, a wealthy town merchant. His father offered to buy him anything he wanted. Père Murray suggested the idea that, since his father was French and his mother English, something to commemorate the "bonne-entente" between the two cultures here in Penetanguishene, Quebec and Ontario should be erected. Thus, two large, magnificent, bronze angels, one marked "Quebec" and the other "Ontario" were unveiled at the main entrance to the town. Many bronze plaques were also unveiled around town during "Old Home Week". This event was marked by media stories across the province.

Also unveiled at this time, amid much pomp, was the LeCaron statue to be placed in front of the church.

This photo shows the massive crowds that came to St. Anne's for the unveiling of the LeCaron statue, during Old Home Week in 1921.

It must have also been a busy time for Père Brunelle as well, as no doubt he was involved in all of the week's festivities. In October, he wrote the Archbishop in French, requesting a two-week vacation in November. He suggested to his superior, a replacement in Father Cabana from the Seminary or, *"I could make arrangements with Father Kelley of Midland."*

The canonical process for the eight Martyrs of Huronia was begun in 1904 when Archbishop Bégin of Quebec petitioned Rome on their behalf. In 1919, the Archbishops and Bishops of Canada again petitioned Rome. On Sunday, June 21st, 1925, Brébeuf and his seven companions were beatified in Rome by Pope Pius XI. They were now declared "Blessed".

Penetanguishene had always had an interest in the Martyrs and the old site of Sainte Marie. In 1852, Reverend George Hallen, the Anglican rector of St. James-on-the-Lines Church, the Establishment's church in Penetanguishene, had visited the old fort and done detailed drawings. In 1855, he and Jesuit Father Félix Martin made extensive measurements and sketches. In 1894, Père Laboureau had bought the property with the intention of turning it over to the Jesuits but due to confusion as to true ownership of the original land, later sold it.

In 1906, the parish of Waubaushene was

Père Gérald Lahaie. He was the boy who entered the Jesuit order and was the reason "the Angels" were donated to the town by his father in 1921.

An early drawing of the North American Martyrs, beatified by Pope Pius XI in Rome, on June 21st, 1925. On that date, they were declared "blessed".

given to the Jesuits. Its new pastor, Père Jean Baptiste Nolin, built a small shrine near the suspected site of martyrdom of Brébeuf and Lalement. As one of three very strong, active voices in the devotion to the eight martyrs, Père Nolin arranged many pilgrimages in Waubaushene and to New York State, and Penetanguishene. When authenticity of the Waubaushene site came into question in 1918, attention turned again to the old fort, where many masses and observances had been held over the years.

Proximity and interest in Sainte Marie can be the only reason why, in the summer of 1925, the Jesuit Provincial, Father M. J. Filion, decided to build a new Shrine in Midland, on the banks near the old fort. It was opened in 1926, with some of the lumber donated by the Beck brothers here in Penetanguishene.

The fact that there was a Jesuit Memorial Church, a "National Shrine", in nearby Penetanguishene, seemed to have been an unorthodox situation for Father Filion, Director of the Shrine in Midland and he was testy about it. In March of 1927, W. F. Beck was a driving force for the Town of Penetanguishene developing a new tourism brochure. In wanting to promote the area, Beck wrote to Father Filion to seek permission to include a reference to the Martyrs' Shrine in nearby Midland. The strong reply came a week later, some of which included the following ill-informed sentiments,

"My difficulty is, that if the Shrine is mentioned in connection with Penetanguishene,

people will be misdirected, and will go to Penetang instead of Midland. The Jesuits were never in Penetang, as far as we know. Father LeCaron was not a Jesuit, and no Jesuit has or ever had anything to do with the so-called Jesuit Memorial Church in your town.

"To be candid with you, it is difficult for me to see how any reference to the Shrine is 'à propos' . . . If I approve of its being included in your pamphlet as belonging to Penetang, then I am treating Midland as if it were a suburb of your town, and you know what trouble may come of this."

Though the Midland Shrine did end up being included in the Penetanguishene brochure, (its distance away had to be clearly

William Beck in front of the family General Store and Lumber Office on Burke Street, now called the Centennial Museum. He saw the benefits of tourism and the history of the town.
Courtesy Penetanguishene Centennial Museum.

stated at the insistence of Father Filion), his comments seemed harsh, coming from someone who had observed and partook of Penetanguishene's Tercentenary Celebrations a mere six years earlier, at the invitation of Père Murray. Why this grand National Shrine here was to be pushed into insignificance was baffling.

Regardless, in Rome, on June 29th,

This is the section of the Penetanguishene tourism pamphlet that advertised the Midland Martyrs' Shrine as a distinct entity away from its neighbouring town, at the request of Father Filion.

1930, before 60,000 faithful, Pope Pius XI proclaimed the eight Martyrs of Huronia to be "Saints".

Nonetheless and regardless of the issue raised concerning the Martyrs, parish business at St. Anne's went on as usual. In October of 1930, Père Brunelle sent the Chancellery a short, interesting letter:

"After inquiring in the neighboring parishes from Barrie to North, I cannot find one who intends to have confirmation this year. Here, we expect to have about 80 children."

The parish was still growing!

Around 1933, Père Brunelle became quite ill, yet in spite of his condition continued as pastor of the parish, aided by Father Flanagan and Father Charles McKinnon as administrators.

During the third decade of this century changes in curates included the names of Fathers James J. Reddin, W.D. Muckle, D. McNamara, H.J. McHenry, Arthur Jacob, and Charles A. McKinnon. The latter remained as curate until 1936 when he became administrator until 1938. Father F. J. Flanagan also came as curate for a time in 1930 and returned for a period of three years from 1933 as ad-

Due to the illness of Père Brunelle, Father Charles MacKinnon became Administrator of the parish 1936-1938.

ministrator. Father W. R. Morrison was a very popular assistant during the year he stayed in Penetanguishene beginning in July, 1936.

When Father McKinnon assumed the responsibilities of administrator of the parish, one of the first items on the agenda was to organize a committee to take care of the cemetery. Its members, Mr. Bob Beaulieu, Mr. S. R. Gendron and Mr. Ray Gauthier first made a plea for funds and within two years the cemetery was in excellent shape.

In August of 1936, Father McKinnon wrote the Chancellery:

" So officially I ask permission to establish 'La Congrégation des Dames de Sainte Anne' in this parish and to affiliate it with the Archem fraternity of Sainte Anne de Beaupré."

Sincerely in Christ,

Chas. A. MacKinnon

P.S. Full title of the church is Sainte Anne's Jesuit Memorial Church

The town was hit hard by casualties during the First World War and the losses affected it deeply. The following was a list of those who offered the supreme sacrifice:

WAR OF 1914 - 1918

Noble Braden, Isaac Beauchamp, Herman Desroches
Joseph Dubeau, George Dusome, Carl Dusome
C. T. Darling, W. T. Elliott, Charles Hirst
Clifford Hames, Wm. Kennedy, Xavier Longlade
Wilfred Morin, A. T. McFadden, Cory Norton
Hal Osborne, John L. Peacock, Napoleon Picotte
E. F. Richardson, F.J. Richardson, Robert Rumble
George Simmons, Harold Sproule, A. H. Thompson
A. L. Webster, A. P. Vasseur, Wilfred Vasseur
J. Vaillancourt, C. Heber Wright, George Morin

From 1933 to 1938, Père Brunelle's health was not good, yet he carried on as Pastor. Finally, he seceded to his friend and fellow-priest, Père Jean-Marie Castex, in September, 1938. From that time, Père Brunelle lived in his newly-constructed house across from the Church on Robert Street. It was a fitting close to a long and useful life that he, who had helped others so generously, should receive the Last Sacraments from the hands of his successor in 1944 at age 67. His memory was a source of inspiration to others for many years after his passing.

The Penetanguishene that Père Brunelle had known so well, was making progress from the days when her economy relied heavily on the lumber industry. Whereas her waterfront was once filled with sawmills, tugs, log booms and box factories, she expanded to include the railway, a tannery, a stove factory and a shipyard, to name a few things. Her Main Street bustled with hotels, butcher shops, drugstores, blacksmith shops, livery stables and more.

But as the thirties brought its own set of hardships, and the great depression took hold, the church of the Martyrs and her priests continued to be a rock of faith to her parishioners and her town.

The Cenotaph on Main Street, built as a tribute to those who had fallen defending freedom in the Great Wars.

Père Jean Marie Castex.
9th Pastor of St. Anne's Parish 1938-1969

7

For The Love Of Mary

The new pastor of St. Anne's Parish, Jean Marie Castex, was born in the small village of Sacoue, Hautes Pyrenées near Lourdes in southern France, in the diocese of Tarbes, on July 22nd, 1871. In 1878, at the age of seven, he was taken by his mother to the small Shrine at Lourdes where he was consecrated to the Blessed Virgin Mary, twenty years after the apparitions to St. Bernadette in 1858.

Having decided to enter the priesthood, he had just finished his classical studies course and was ready for his debut in philosophy in 1890, when French law intervened in his life. At this time, all young French men had to give three years of military training, an edict with no exception for those who were studying for the priesthood. With a full realization of the consequences, Jean Castex took the law into his own hands and by the time the authorities got around to ask where the boy was, they learned he was continuing his studies for the priesthood in Canada.

Ordained on May 30, 1896, by Archbishop Duhamel in the Basilica in Ottawa, Père Castex served in various capacities in several dioceses like Ottawa, Kingston, Victoria in British Columbia and finally Brooklyn, New York, over the next fourteen years. Finally, he was requested by Archbishop McEvay to work in the diocese of Toronto. After working under Dean Hand in St. Paul's, from whom he learned a great deal of Pastoral Theology, Père Castex, in 1913, was invited to a professorial chair at the newly-opened St. Augustine's Seminary in Scarborough. There he taught Gregorian Chant, Liturgy and French Literature for the next eight years. He was also the Seminary's first Bursar.

Even at this young age and early in his church career, Père Castex was strong-willed. Monsignor John Kidd, a former priest here at St. Anne's, was the first Rector of the new Seminary. One day, Père Castex and Monsignor Kidd had a falling out as to the manner Père was keeping the books. With their rooms across the hall from one another, the young priest collected his accounting books and proceeded across the hall and threw them on the floor in front of the Rector's office.

Hearing the racket, Monsignor Kidd opened the door to discover a steaming Castex in front of him.

"If you don't like the way that I'm doing business, then do it yourself!" With that he stormed off in front of the astonished Kidd, who would himself go on to be a bishop.

From 1921 to 1930, Père Castex was assigned to St. Margaret's Parish in Midland where he was instrumental in establishing the Separate Schools. The bells in the church there were also the result of his efforts. During the depression years, Père Castex was stationed in Phelpston, a mainly Irish parish then, just north of Barrie.

Standing about five feet, eight inches in height, rather sturdily built, he was a human dynamo with a keen wit. With his presence, the parish would be blessed with another builder.

Arriving in September of 1938 as pastor of St. Anne's Parish, he opened St. David's Chapel across the Bay on the first Sunday of Advent, December 4th of that same year.

On April 8th of 1941, he wrote to Father Callaghan at the Chancellery to ask its permission to build a community vault in order to store the deceased bodies through the winter months.

"Naturally we have to be in it," he wrote but quickly added, *"The Church is not going to spend any money towards that work . . . You should see our church at night with all the lights on. It's beautiful. But you will see it soon again - the snow is practically gone!"*

The next year, he wrote the Chancellery again with an innovative idea for the parish, even though it was a common Catholic tradition.

"We have decided to hold a Novena of Holy Hours beginning on Sunday, April 12th and closing Sunday, June 7th with the customary procession of the Blessed Sacrament. This is quite an undertaking. The purpose of that public supplication is to obtain God's protection on our soldiers and a lasting peace with justice.

"The non-Catholics of the town as well as our people will be invited to attend these devotions. And we intend to make them as solemn as we can to make them more fervent . . . Very likely the Holy Hour will be from 4 to 5 p.m. so

St. David's Chapel or Church. Located across the bay, the one-story building was opened in December of 1938, and remained this way until renovations added a top floor in 1962.

Novena of Holy Hours house decorated with flowers for procession with children dressed as angels or carrying baskets of flower petals.

as not to interfere with Protestant services . . . We expect the Archbishop for Confirmation this spring, and at the same time to preside at the closing service June 7th . . . " Then, at the end of his letter he added rather ruefully:

" I have the maple syrup, but this time Joe Marchildon is charging higher prices. I had him from $2.75 to $2.65 per gallon . . . it is high but I think that is the best we can do!"

On September 21st, 1942, a local disaster occurred with the sinking of Corbeau's yacht, "Wawinte" near Beausoleil Island. Twenty-five men drowned that night, including the ship's owner, Bert Corbeau, an NHL legend in Penetanguishene. The disaster hit Penetanguishene and Midland very hard. News of it travelled far and wide and prompted the Archbishop of Toronto, Cardinal McGuigan to write Père Castex the very next day.

"Please accept my very sincere sympathy in the great loss sustained by the unfortunate accident in Georgian Bay by which twenty-five lost their lives, some of these from your own parish. Please be good enough to extend my personal sympathy to the bereaved families and assure them that I will offer Mass for their loved ones and pray for the repose of their immortal souls."

In 1943, Père had the old altar remodeled at St. Anne's with a new Tabernacle, and enlarged the sanctuary with a new sacristy, store-room and stairs leading down to the basement. He also updated the rectory with new wiring, heating, and floors. A new kitchen addition enabled the rectory to accommodate a visiting Bishop or Cardinal without one of the curates having to find another place to sleep for the night.

Cardinal James McGuigan, Archbishop of Toronto.

Père Castex was not done. Both the church and rectory were repainted as well as a 100 yard wall constructed to form a terrace along Robert Street. Fred Laurin broke through three feet of stone to install a new side entrance to the church along with new landscaping.

The Hall in the church basement was redecorated and named in memory of Père Laboureau. Then he turned his attention to building a camp called "Marygrove", eight miles outside of the town and located on the other side of Penetanguishene Bay across from the reformatory. Built at that time as a retreat for the children of the parish, it housed a chapel-recreation hall, dining room and sleeping quarters.

The cemetery property was extended and larger recreational grounds for the school added. Next, Monsignor Castex's gaze focused on replacing the town's small, antiquated hospital, for which he was responsible for having the Grey Sisters-of-the-Immaculate-Conception of Pembroke put in charge. Property beside the old one was purchased and planning was begun in earnest.

In 1946, Pope Pius XII conferred upon Père Castex the title of Domestic Prelate or "Monsignor", just before he celebrated the Golden Jubilee of his ordination to the Holy Priesthood.

The Monsignor was a going concern throughout the town in his day. *"Sermons must be easy to understand and as interesting as you can make them,"* was his credo. He made a point of visiting all nine hundred and fifteen families in the parish every year.

Missions were held at the parish periodically as in 1944, when Father Augustine C.P. gave a week's mission to the young people and a year later, he returned with Father Nagle, C.P. for a two week stay. In 1947, the parish received the visitation of the Statue of Our Lady of Fatima. That same year a new wooden cupola was built to cover the bells. It was constructed by Albert, Majoric and Claude Brunelle and was finished on August 6th, 1947.

Also in 1947, Monsignor Castex began planning in earnest for a new addition to be added to the old hospital to honour the veterans of the war. Monsignor Castex had even involved Cardinal McGuigan in his plans. On March 20th, the Cardinal wrote Castex:

"I . . . give you the permission required to donate $1,000.00 from Parish Funds to this work . . . I will also give $1,000.00.

" . . . How about the Old People's Home? I have been thinking about it and wondering if there was any advancement in plans."

Six days later, on March 26th, 1947, a "Recognition Dinner" was held to honour those veterans who had served in the 2nd World War and returned home, and to also recognize those who did not return.

Monsignor Castex addressed the crowd that night in the basement of the church in Laboureau Hall, where many blood donor clinics had been held to give blood to help wounded soldiers during the war.

" . . . Above all," Castex told the hushed crowd, *"Thirty-five of the flowers of our youth have made the supreme sacrifice, - with their lives they have given all: their bright future, the welfare of their families, the expectations of their country . . .*

"They have sacrificed all. Here my friends, the words of Holy Writ come to mind, 'Greater love than this no one has, that one lay down his life for his friends.'

" . . . At this solemn moment all I can say is God bless you eternally, children, for the life you have given us through your death. Thanks to the parents of these victims. They deserve our deep and heartfelt gratitude."

The crowd stood in sorrowful attention as Monsignor Castex read aloud slowly and solemnly, the names of the fallen. Many in the hall wept. It was a poignant moment in the town's history.

This early picture taken shortly after it's official opening, clearly shows the large wooden stairs that graced the front of the church. Also note there are no bells.

St. Anne's Jesuit Memorial Church, with her bells and cupola.

73

WAR OF 1939 - 1945

Murray Allen, Fred Atkins, Eric Booth
Peter Brasseur, Joseph Cloutier,
William Cloutier, Donald Copeland, Hugh Curry,
Aldie Desrochers, Raymond Dion,
Léonard Desjardins Raymond Dupuis,
Robert Dubeau, Norman Frazeau, Francis Forget,
Patrick Garraway, Garnet Hopper,
Léo Lacroix, Raymond Lacroix,
Lawrence Legault, Lionel Leroux,
Russell McIntaggart, Philip Maher,
Charles Marshall, Ronald Noble,
Willard Perrault, René Quesnelle, Philbert Robillard,
Frank Rogers, Robert Sawyer,
Douglas Webster, James Yelland

only two weeks when Cardinal MacGuigan appointed him to Penetanguishene for the summer months in June of 1949. Originally from Toronto, he had been sent by the Cardinal to study at "Le Grand Séminaire" at Laval in Quebec City. He emerged fluently bilingual and ideal to help out in a bilingual parish. He recalled his arrival like it had occurred just yesterday.

"It was a Saturday, when I showed up at the Rectory, met by Monsignor Castex at the door. Robert Street was closed as there was a church bazaar going on. He immediately asked me for my letter of appointment to make sure I was "bona fida". Then he said, 'You will have to take care of your own supper, then you will hear confessions at 7:30.' There, just like that.

"He struck me that first weekend as someone who was very much in charge and not at all impressed with a young priest, 24 years or so of age, who had arrived carrying his golf clubs!

"That night I met the other priests, Frank Sullivan, Joe O'Neill and Louis Dignard, whom I had met when I entered the seminary in 1942 as he was a deacon then. There was a great awe and respect for deaconal students. I had always had great respect for him, and so to arrive in '49 and Louis Dignard was there, well I felt better right away. At least I knew somebody!

"But I enjoyed Penetang! I had never been to such a small town before. To be in that part of the diocese was very impressionable on me. I found the people to be unbelievably friendly and welcoming."

He went on later to suggest that a wing be added to the old hospital in memory of the men and then read aloud Cardinal McGuigan's letter of support. It was from these years after the war that the community's thoughts, inspired by Monsignor Castex, turned to improving our hospital facilities, which would bear fruition many years later.

From 1938 to 1949, the curates sent to assist Monsignor Castex consisted of Fathers John McGoey, R. Walsh (of St. Francis Xavier Foreign Mission Society), Sid Howe, Joseph O'Neill, Frank E. Sullivan, John Kelly and Pères Louis J. Dignard, Stanislas Paradis, Philip Bouvier, and Armand Desaulniers.

In 1949, the Redemptorist Fathers gave the "Parish Retreat" as well.

Leonard J. Wall, a future Archbishop of Winnipeg, was a priest

Bishop Leonard J. Wall as he appeared in the 1980's, was originally sent to St. Anne's in June of 1949 as a summer assignment. He maintained a long relationship and contact with the parish, especially as Chancellor of the Archdiocese.

That September found the young Wall in Rome furthering his studies and returning in 1950 to resume responsibilities as Secretary to Cardinal McGuigan. By this time, Leonard Wall's good friend and classmate, Father John Kelly, who had been ordained alongside him in St. Michael's Cathedral, was Monsignor Castex's curate. Wall's knowledge of and association with St. Anne's would only continue and intensify in 1954.

"In 1954, a staff member at St. Augustine's (in Toronto) became ill," he recalls, *"and the Cardinal sent me to fill in. The first phone call I received was from Monsignor Castex, who said quite matter-of-factly, 'Now that you are teaching at the Seminary, you will come here to Penetanguishene for the summers. You will be useful!' That was the beginning of eight or nine years in succession of summers in Penetang. I had courses to prepare for the fall but I was there as a summer assistant.*

"I got to know the countryside very well, often visiting Father

Armand Desaulniers in Perkinsfield and Thomas Marchildon in Lafontaine, who thought I was a 'real Catholic' because I could speak French just as well as he could!

"Père Castex, as we called him, had great faith, and devotion to the Virgin Mary. We would say the beads, the Rosary, at table after every evening meal. The housekeeper would come in from the kitchen after the meal and we'd go - 'Bon, envoie fort!'

"In those years, I found the practice of the faith strong. People were attached to the sacraments such as confession. I remember we would hear confessions all through the week but especially so on Saturdays, and for hours at a time. And there were great devotions to St. Anne. I can recall conducting a Novena for the feast of St. Anne with the choir and everything. I believe the parish was inspired by the example of Père Castex."

The summer of 1954 was an especially busy summer for the parish as Père Marchildon of Lafontaine preached the sermon at a mass celebrating the Marian Year on July 15th. The New Penetanguishene General Hospital was officially opened on July 25th and the Blessing of the Hospital's new Stations of the Cross by the Very Reverend Dean Clair of Barrie on August 19th. The next day on August 20th, the latest and newest "Champlain Cross", constructed by the Knight's of Columbus at Picotte's Point, was blessed by Father Wall.

Sunday, August 22nd, would be an especially busy day, as the new hospital was officially blessed in an afternoon ceremony

This photo was taken on the afternoon of the dedication of the new Champlain Cross at Toanché on August 20th, 1954. It was blessed by Father Wall.

by Monsignor Callaghan of Toronto. Known for his devotion to the Virgin Mary, Père Castex also had a small replica of the Lourdes Grotto in France, where the Virgin Mary had reportedly appeared to a peasant girl named Bernadette Soubirous, built beside the church. Inspired by Roy Patenaude, Chairman of the Grotto Committee, it was built by Alex Gravelle and Herb Carrière, with assistance from Jules Vallée, Marc Picotte, Ted Leblanc, Eugène Quesnelle, Raymond Emery, Eldège Quesnelle, Albert Vallée, and Ed Tessier.

It was dedicated and blessed in an impressive ceremony that Sunday evening, with Monsignor McQuillen of St. Catherines giving the sermon. Then Monsignor Callaghan blessed the cornerstone and statues. In fact,

the cornerstone was a piece of stone taken directly from the very grotto at Massabielle where St. Bernadette had seen the vision of the Virgin Mary. The Rock of Lourdes was then venerated.

On August 29th, Monsignor Castex blessed the new cross at the cemetery.

At long last, in 1955, at a ceremony in Barrie, Ontario, Monsignor 'Père' Jean Marie Castex became an official Canadian citizen.

Father Louis Bourque was another priest sent to help Monsignor Castex and was involved in the Young People's Club in the parish. In December of 1959, the Club, through Father Bourque, asked the Archdiocese for permission to distribute a card that would be titled:

"The Teen Commandments."

1. Stop and think before you drink.
2. Don't let your parents down - they brought you up.
3. Be humble enough to obey - you will be giving orders yourself someday.
4. At the first moment, turn away from unclean thinking.
5. Don't show off when driving - if you want to race, go to a race track.
6. Choose a date who would make a good mate.
7. Go to church faithfully - the Creator gives you the week; give Him back an hour.
8. Choose your companions carefully - you are what they are.
9. Avoid following the crowd - be a leader and not just a follower.
10. Or even better - keep the original Ten Commandments.

Monsignor Castex' Grotto. Built beside the church in 1954, it's cornerstone was taken directly from the grotto built at Lourdes, France. *Photos courtesy of Archdiocese of Toronto Archives.*

The priests of the parish played an integral part of the activities of the youth, and through other social activities as this picture demonstrates.

In March of 1960, a language war erupted in the town and the parish. In the middle of it was Monsignor Jean Marie Castex.

Despite the fact that he was from France, Monsignor clearly favoured the use of English at church and schools, despite the fact that over 80% of the Penetanguishene population and an even higher majority of his parishioners spoke French as a first language. This was even reflected in the name change on all church letterhead, from the French "Ste Anne's" to the English "St. Ann's". Under his charge, most masses and Sacraments were in English, which finally resulted in a very public backlash.

When he opposed the formation of a French Parent-Teacher Association, even getting the support of Cardinal McGuigan, he was sent an anonymous letter in which he was branded a "Judas."

This 1957 photo of the marriage of Ted and Marie Light clearly shows the old pulpit and the painting of the resurrected Christ which was later painted over by a painting of the marriage of Mary and Joseph in the 1960 renovations.

This photo shows Monsignor Castex bowling at the Knights of Columbus Hall, an activity which he loved and did despite his advancing years. It was a true indication of his vigour.

The affair hit the papers, even appearing in The Toronto Star.

Although 89 years of age at this time, Monsignor vigorously defended himself:

"That hurt! And I'll continue to favour English. I am convinced the opposition is out to make the town 100% French!

"That would be alright in Quebec, but this is Ontario, where English is the main language. I know of many cases of children leaving our schools and either failing to get or losing jobs because of their poor English."

Monsignor went on to point his finger at the Brothers, known as "les Frères du Sacré-Coeur", and the Sisters, "les Soeurs de Sainte Croix", who taught in the three French Public Catholic schools, for supporting the conflict. Even his Assistants didn't always agree with his methods. This situation came to an almost comical head one Sunday when Père Joseph Marchand filled in for Monsignor Castex and said all the readings and sermons in French. To say that upon his return Monsignor was not impressed would be an understatement!

"After I had arrived, Monsignor asked me about it," Père Louis Dignard recalls, *"the French-English problems that he had become embroiled in earlier. I answered that I thought we were here to serve all the people, that we shouldn't favour one over the other, that it was too divisive. We were here to serve and prac-*

tise the faith. He finally came around and allowed the Saturday night Mass to be said in French and it gradually became evenly distributed between French and English. He eventually softened but it took a while."

But to many, it was a bitter period in the church's history and the repercussions would fester twenty years later over the fight for a French language high school.

Still, Père Castex was not done beautifying his church. The local headlines read, *"Several hundred persons of all faiths attend 'open house' at St. Anne's - See works of beauty".* On November 13th, 1960, he invited the whole community to an "open house" to see the extensive restoration and expansion work done to the church. The church overflowed with guests who received guided

This 1961 photo clearly shows the front of the church as it looked just after the major 1960 Renovations and re-painting.

tours of the new west addition. It housed the new St. John's Baptistry, and below it, St. Cecilia's Hall, to be used for small meetings. Pamphlets describing all the paintings, windows and statues in the church were also handed out.

It was truly a major refurbishing as visitors were awed by the remodeled altar with its new communion rail and pulpit, all constructed of ornate Italian marble. For the first time, the community saw a stunning mosaic of the Last Supper installed below the altar.

Three new murals were painted on the ceiling of this Shrine by Italian painters, Joseph Valerio and his brother, Gaetano from London, Ont. The closest painting at the back is a beautiful portrait of the eight North American Martyrs, the center one depicts Saint Anne, holding baby Mary, while the front one is of "Saint Bernadette" Soubirous experiencing her vision of the Virgin Mary at Lourdes, France in 1858.

The Valerio brothers also repainted and touched up the other murals. On the west wall near the front, a new mural depicting the wedding of Joseph and Mary was painted over a mural of Christ. Again, Monsignor Castex's strong affection to the Virgin Mary is evident in this last round of works he accomplished. At the very front new murals were painted of Jesus and Mary, and over the altar a huge mural was added of the Holy Trinity in Heaven.

In August of 1961, Monsignor Castex wrote to the Coadjutor Archbishop of Toronto, Phillip Pocock, reporting that his work in the parish was pretty well complete.

"*The portables for the High School are ready . . . St. Joseph's Chapel (Marygrove Camp) and surroundings done also . . . That means some money required. . . $10,000.00 supposed to be given . . . the summer collections there . . . will repay that amount.*"

The cheque was sent with a letter thanking him for his years of service, for the camp and its services for area children. It should be noted as well that Monsignor also had a cottage beside the Marygrove camp, where he often retreated for respite and peace during the summer months. This practice always caused a little disorganization at the Rectory as Monsignor always took the housekeeper with him to Marygrove for the summer as well.

The church across the bay was never forgotten either during Castex's stewardship. Volunteers had painted the inside and outside of the building in 1953 and then paid $150.00 to have its exterior painted two years later. In the Fall of 1961, Monsignor Castex spoke to the congregation of St. David's Church about raising funds to add a top story with a new roof.

The fundraising campaign at St. David's began in earnest in December of 1961 and in April of 1962, construction began. On Sunday, July 1st, 1962, Archbishop Pocock blessed the renovated church

The mission church across the bay, Our Lady of the Rosary, formerly St. David's, as she looks today with her second story added in 1962. She has always had a 9:30 mass every Sunday.

Herb Boucher, longtime caretaker of the mission church across the bay.

and then said Mass in the upstairs for the first time.

On July 15th Monsignor announced, *"This Church is now dedicated to Our Lady of the Rosary and will no longer be called St. David's. The hall downstairs will be called St. David's Hall."* A week later, Mr. And Mrs. Antoine Grozelle and family were thanked for donating the money to purchase the statue of the "Sacred Heart."

In 1972, the parishioners of The Our Lady of the Rosary Church erected a picture of Herb Boucher, the caretaker of the church during her first 34 years. Pat Marcille has been the loyal caretaker for the past twenty-nine years.

Increasingly, priests were sent to St Anne's to help with the parish. From 1949 through 1964 were Fathers Lawrence McGough, Gabriel Brien, Leo Ramsperger, Leonard O'Malley, James Keelor, C.J. Dougherty and Pères Léo Perusse, Charles Gagné, Guy Hamel, and Joseph Marchand. And in the summer months came one Leonard Wall, who recalled, *"because of my friendship with Father Kelly and Monsignor Castex, Penetanguishene was always a rectory where I could go to relax."*

By this time though, it was apparent that Monsignor's age and health were finally catching up with him. Having been instrumental in helping save the Penetanguishene General Hospital in 1942 when it was bankrupt, he engineered a plan that not only built a new hospital in 1954 but in turn handed the hospital's ownership and administration over to the Grey Sisters-of-the-Immaculate-Conception of Pembroke. Many credit him for having saved the town's hospital. In need of medical care now, the Sisters in turn provided the Chaplain's room for him and cared for him.

This arrangement was evident when Father John Kelly was canonically appointed the Apostolic Administrator of the parish with full powers. Upon receiving the news by letter, it was with a heavy heart that he had to go up to the General Hospital to break the news to Père, his mentor, whom he loved dearly.

Leaving the rectory, he stopped at the bank to present his newly appointed authori-

zation and to transfer the signing authority. He then proceeded up to the hospital to break the news to his ailing but proud, and still strong-minded Pastor. Père's first reply was, *"Have you been to the bank yet?"*

"Well . . . yes." His curate answered shyly. Monsignor Castex nodded. *"I knew you would"* he said, *"I don't like it but it's the right thing to do!"*

Now the acting administrator of the parish, Father Kelly sent the spiritual reports of St. Anne's and the church across the bay, still referred to in records as St. David's Mission, to the Archdiocese on March 13th, 1962. In it he stated:

"Monsignor Castex is remaining about the same. He has been moved from his hospital room down to his own room in the hospital and says mass when it is not too long. He said mass this morning and there were no ill effects. He had an electrocardiograph taken recently and the report came back that he was normal."

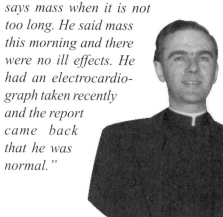

Father John Kelly, priest here at St. Anne's from 1949-1964, was the acting administrator of the parish for the last two of those years due to the illness of Monsignor Castex.

In September of the same year, Father Kelly wrote to Chancellor Fulton asking permission to have Fathers Mann and Rolls preach a mission at St. Anne's and of course ended with:

"The Monsignor has not changed much, he is still at his cottage and plans to move to the hospital this afternoon. However, he has been (saying) this for weeks so we will believe it when we see it."

In his response, Monsignor Fulton added:

" No doubt the advent of cooler weather may occasion Monsignor's moving back to the hospital. As you probably know, we did obtain the Indult from the Holy See so that he could say Mass sitting down."

On February 5th of 1963, Father Kelly sent this report:

" I am enclosing a cheque for the Catholic Immigrants Collection which amounted to $239.42.

"The Monsignor had another coronary last Saturday afternoon. He said mass on Thursday and stood all the way through it. He made a few visits around the parish last week as well, so I suppose the whole week was just too much for him. He has had the hiccups since yesterday afternoon but this has happened before. However, each attack leaves him weaker."

In 1964, Archbishop Philip Pocock had a team assembled to plan and build a new College in Toronto. On his team was Leonard J. Wall. Wall wanted his old friend and classmate, John Kelly, to come to the college to be the first Bursar. Having been under the tutelage of Monsignor Castex, he and the Archbishop knew that Kelly would bring a strong pastoral influence to the new school. But it would be a decision that would demonstrate the influence and respect that Monsignor Castex still possessed. Today, the retired Archbishop of Winnipeg, Leonard Wall recalls:

An impressive group of 52 Altar Boys posing for a 1946 photo.   *Courtesy of Raymond Vaillancourt.*

"Archbishop Pocock said, 'I don't have the heart to ask him (Castex) to give up John. So you go up to negotiate with Monsignor Castex and see if you can get Father Kelly.' And so I did. The negotiations went well. Père Castex was a great churchman. He had a great devotion to the seminary and the shaping of young men for the priesthood. He knew that Father Kelly could contribute to that. Besides, it was his Archbishop's request. He was assured that he would be sent someone he would be comfortable with."

Indeed he was, in the person of Père Louis Dignard.

"I received a letter informing me of my transfer to Penetanguishene as Associate Pastor, and that I was to 'assist' Monsignor Castex as much as possible," recalled Père Dignard, who would come here for a second and permanent stint, beginning in 1964.

"Not knowing quite what 'as much as possible' meant," he continues, *"I called the Chancellery to find out exactly what my appointment entailed, its wording made me a little unsure. 'Well,' they said, 'you are to pretty well run the parish, and maybe you could inform or consult with Monsignor now and then."*

On Sunday, August 15th, 1965, a new plaque was unveiled in an impressive ceremony at the Champlain Cross on Penetanguishene Bay at Picotte's Point. The Huronia Council of the Knights of Columbus had the plaque constructed. It was unveiled by William Davis, Ontario Minister of Education, and dedicated by Monsignor Castex. Mayor Mary Rogers was the Master of Ceremonies.

Present at the ceremony was Dr. P.B. Rynard, M.P.; Simcoe County Warden Herb Hughes; Midland Mayor Herb Beauchamp, and Tiny Reeve Montcalm Maurice. Midland historian, Herbert Cranston introduced the guest speaker, Mrs. Elsie Jury, who was the wife of archaeologist Dr. Wilfred Jury and was a noted historian in her own right. Mrs. Jury began her extensive talk about Champlain and his travels with the remark that she felt highly honoured to be standing at this historical spot.

The bilingual plaque read:

"Penetanguishene-
Samuel de Champlain
Father of French Canada, landed here on August 1ˢᵗ, 1615,
during his explorations of Huronia."

This drawing of the Champlain Plaque that was unveiled the afternoon of August 15th, 1965, near the Toanché Cross, coincided with the 350th anniversary of the landing of Champlain and the first mass celebrated by Père LeCaron.

That afternoon, a crowd of 2000 people attended the 350ᵗʰ Anniversary Mass at Carhagouha, which celebrated the arrival of Champlain and the first mass celebrated by Père Joseph LeCaron there in 1615. Archbishop Pocock was the celebrant with five monsignors and eight priests in attendance. Monsignor Alphonse Bélanger preached the sermon.

Monsignor Jean Marie Castex wasn't leaving the stage just yet either. On May 12ᵗʰ, 1966, he concelebrated a Mass to mark the 70ᵗʰ anniversary of his ordination to the priesthood. It was an extraordinary milestone!

He continued to live in his hospital room at the Penetanguishene General, but with each passing year, his trips to his beloved cottage beside the Marygrove camp became less frequent.

As a sign of respect, Monsignor Castex was never fully or "officially" relieved as Pastor here, becoming *Pastor Emeritus* in 1969. As he neared his 100ᵗʰ birthday, he was quiet and at peace.

"Even when he was on his bed, you know, near the end, his life slipping away," recalls Dignard today, *"I would go and sit with him and talk about the parish, what was going on and it made him feel like he was*

On May 12th, 1966, Monsignor Castex celebrated 70 years in the priesthood, as this photo captures the special concelebration mass held that day.

still a part of it. I still feel he had a deep influence on me. I was most struck by his deep faith."

Monsignor Castex was cared for to the end by the Sisters at 'his' hospital and died quietly there on February 27th, 1971, five months shy of his 100th birthday.

His Funeral Mass at St Anne's on Wednesday, March 3rd, was one of the largest Penetanguishene had seen in years. She bid good-bye again to another of her faithful servants.

Monsignor Leonard J. Wall, an old friend, felt at the outset that Père Marchildon should give the homily. Archbishop Pocock nodded understandingly but insisted that Père Castex was deserving of having the Chancellor of the Archdiocese speak at his funeral and so Wall was the homilist.

"Nothing was more a part of Père Castex's life than prayer," Wall told the packed church that day. *"He believed in the power of prayer because he was consumed with an intense dedication to the glory of God.*

" . . . To ask outright for wisdom or for anything else was typical of him. . . God's ways he thought to be direct. Twenty years ago, when he was persistently trying to convince Cardinal McGuigan to approve plans for the new hospital, he would say to His Eminence in parting at the close of each unsuccessful encounter: 'If you won't say yes, don't say no.'

"The 'no' was never pronounced: for that matter nobody ever heard the 'yes' either, but the Penetanguishene General Hospital stands as a tribute to the tireless dedication of this great priest, who was then ten years past today's retirement age of seventy.

"He accepted commitment to service as the portion of his inheritance in the priesthood of Christ. The 30th day of May this year would have crowned 75 years of service to those to whom he was sent in the place of Christ and in the name of the Church. Having lived to his hundredth year, his renown will be legend."

Another large chapter in the parish book of St. Anne's was inexorably closed.

Monsignor Jean Marie Castex
1871-1971

82

Frère Alex F.S.C. and Soeur
Charles-André S.S.C.J.

8

Of Schools, Brothers and Sisters

From the moment the Ontario school system was established, the schools, whether frequented by a heavily Catholic population or not, were public schools due to the grant system. Separate school grants came into being only many years later. With a predominantly French-Catholic influx of immigrants to the town when it was being established, it was only natural that her early public schools reflected this. And, in Catholic pockets where schools were burgeoning, their development was always accompanied by members of various religious orders whose strong teaching skills intertwined with Catholic, public education throughout the country. St. Anne's Parish was no exception.

In 1845, a log public school was constructed at the corner of Owen and Robert Street, and named "School Section No. 1 for Tiny and Tay". It remained in use until 1874 when the first brick school was built on the same site. It was named like the parish, St. Anne's. A brick building with rounded windows, fancy gables and a belfry at the

St. Anne's Public School, located at the corner of Owen and Robert Streets, was first constructed in 1874. By the time this photo was taken in 1881, the school was already overcrowded, with classes being squeezed into the old town hall.

center, it welcomed 49 children in its first year but it soon mushroomed to over 130 students.

With an influx of settlers to the area and a booming population, this school was soon too small and classes were added to the Old Town Hall in 1881. In 1892, the vestry of Père Laboureau's Jesuit Memorial Shrine, still under construction, was hastily completed to hold another class. Also at this time, Père Laboureau, the Secretary-Treasurer of the school, arranged for a Miss Julie Porter to come from London, England to teach music.

The Catholic population must have grown drastically at the turn of the century because a new second story was put on the public school in 1906, with a large and last addition being added to the north side facing Robert Street two years later. This addition, built under the direction of Père Brunet, cost approximately $15,000.00 and easily doubled the size of the school.

In 1918, Père Philippe Brunelle obtained the services of the

By 1906, St. Anne's School had a second story added to meet the educational demands of a growing Catholic population.

In 1908, a large addition was added to the front of the old St. Anne's Public School in an attempt to keep up with an exploding population. It remained in use until 1962, when St Joseph's School was built. *Courtesy of Penetanguishene Centennial Museum.*

Sisters-of-St.-Joseph from Toronto to come to the public school to teach. Their participation in education in the town marked a turning point in Catholic education here.

Until 1927, instruction in all Ontario schools was restricted to English only, but its law, Bill 17, which imposed this restriction, was repealed, so that by 1928, the school here began introducing some classes in French and became officially bilingual. French language instruction began to grow in the school and soon the English classes taught by the Sisters from Toronto became the minority.

By the mid 1930s, it became apparent to the pastor, Père Philippe Brunelle, that the English Sisters needed French assistance and after speaking with Archbishop McGuigan, obtained the services of another order of Sisters, "Les Soeurs-de-Sainte-Croix". Four Sisters came in August of 1935, settling into the convent house at 20 Poyntz Street. They were: Soeur Dominica, Soeur Zélie, Soeur Irène and Soeur Félix. For two years, the two Orders of Sisters worked closely alongside one another, each teaching in their respective languages. At this time, there were 548 students divided among 12 classrooms.

With the number of Sisters being sent to Penetanguishene increasing, they moved into a new convent near the school in 1937. Then suddenly the Sisters-of-St. Joseph were recalled to help in the Toronto region and they departed in July of 1937. Still, they continued to return to the town they had grown so fond of and many of them visited each summer for years afterwards for respite and vacation.

Soon the enlarged school was overflowing and two houses in town were bought and housed classes to take the overflow. Known individually as the "pink" and "white" schools, they were each visited by fire respectively in 1939 and 1942. Despite both schoolhouses being saved by the town fire brigade, the fires prompted the local school board to examine the construction of a new, more centralized school.

During the ravages of the Second World War, when building material and labour were at a premium, a new larger school was built on the same property near Poyntz Street. Opened in January of 1945 and called "Ecole Ste. Croix", it accommodated eleven classrooms - nine bilingual and two

Ecole Ste. Croix was opened in 1945. It had eleven classrooms and at its center was a courtyard/auditorium that doubled as a gymnasium.

English. This new school housed a center courtyard that doubled as an auditorium and a gymnasium with a basketball court. At first it housed only junior grades, with the remainder staying in the old St. Anne's.

A picture taken of the teaching staff of Ecoles St. Anne and Ste. Croix in 1950 showed the influence of religious orders in teaching at that time. Seventeen were nuns and only four were lay people.

A special component of Catholic education in Penetanguishene evolved in 1952. A religious order of Brothers called "Frères-du-Sacré-Coeur", as they were known to the French parishioners, came primarily to become involved with and to teach the boys of the parish and to help in the Catholic schools in both languages. Some were also destined to teach at the old Penetanguishene High School. The Brothers immediately took up residence in the large house, known as the old "white school" next to the church. It became known as the Brothers'

House. They co-existed very well with the Sisters and even had regular meals with them at the convent in their early years.

The impact of the Brothers was immediate as one of them, Frère Alex became the Principal of St. Anne's. With him was Frère Richard. By Christmas, Frère Savio had arrived as well. Their arrival also coincided with the segregation of the boys who stayed

This 1950 photo of the Ste. Croix and St. Anne's teaching staff clearly showed the large numbers of Sisters teaching at the schools. *Courtesy Anne Gagné.*

in the old Ecole St. Anne with the Brothers, and the girls going with the Sisters to Ecole Ste Croix.

Without doubt the main reason the boys got the Brothers was because athleticism was not considered a priority for girls. Sports at that time were purely a "boys" thing, and the Brothers' integration into the lives of their students reflected this.

Former Chair of the School Board, Gil Robillard, recalls:

"At that time in Penetanguishene there were five or six outdoor skating rinks. The Brothers proposed putting a rink up behind the church. The Board thought it was a great idea provided the community had access to it and that there was a limited amount of time given to hockey. We wanted everybody, girls and boys, to be able to skate on it. It worked out pretty well."

Come the first threat of snow, wooden side boards were built to form the rink and the Brothers maintained it all through the winter, involving their young students in this

Gil Robillard was a former chair of the local school board. This was a photo of him when he was Mayor of Penetanguishene between 1966 and 1969.
Courtesy Penetanguishene Centennial Museum.

Brother Anthony was a great hockey player in the Penetang Industrial Hockey League while he was here. He is in the back row, third from left, on the Scott's Sports Shop Canadians, in the early 1960's. *Courtesy of Fred Patterson.*

process as much as possible. But their impact was felt in many other ways.

"The Brothers wanted to start a woodworking shop in the basement of the school," Robillard continues. *"Board member Charlie Martin was dead set against it. But the next thing you know, after five minutes in the basement with the Brothers showing him their plans, Charlie is down at Tessier's Planing Mill buying lumber and tools! He became right involved and was down there with them and everything! Charlie was an engineer by trade and he immediately saw the benefits for the boys."*

By 1956, the Brothers were teaching 423 boys, 254 of them in bilingual classes. Likewise the Sisters were teaching 412 girls with 273 of them getting bilingual instruction.

Alvin Dupuis recalls the impact of the arrival of another Brother, who would succeed Brother Alex as Principal:

"Frère Raynald came here from southern Ontario, Windsor or

Chatham somewhere, where he had one of the best choirs in all of Ontario. They had won many awards and such. So when he came, he started a choir here. All the kids in the school went up to the top floor of the old High School where there was a big room or auditorium, and he tested all the kids for the choir, to see what their range was, how they could sing and where they would fit into the choir.

"We had a good choir. I sang tenor. Brother Anthony or Frère Antoine, he also sang tenor. He had a fantastic voice. We were a good choir, but he topped us off. He made our sound so much better. But we only sang locally, concerts or at the Masses and such, but we were pretty good."

Students recalled Frère Charles as a very serious, fantastically gifted teacher who could write on the chalkboard all day, without a single note in front of him, go into immense detail on any subject and keep his students interested. His knowledge impressed his students and his influence immeasurably lifted their work ethics and their marks.

Frère Donald was described as less serious, more comical but an average teacher. But could the man play hockey. Alvin Dupuis recalls:

"Both Frère Antoine and Frère Donald played hockey in the Industrial League in town. They were both good players but Frère Donald especially so. He was a great player who had an unbelievable slap shot! The goalies were always afraid of his shot!"

It also appears that Frère Antoine, who taught at the Penetanguishene High School, located in the field near present day James Keating School, had a way with keeping the kids off the street and involved in athletics. A former student recalls:

"On Saturday mornings, a bunch of us would go up to the Brother's House to get Brother Anthony to open the High School for us so that we could play basketball and stuff. And he would. We would spend the whole weekend at the High School playing sports with Brother Anthony. He would open it all weekend. It was great!"

Like priests, the Brothers were moved from parish to parish, and from school to school. Brothers who came here at one time or another also included Frères Alex, Martin, Félix, Nicholas, Leonard, Xavier and Mathias, to name a few. It is clear that the presence of the Brothers had an impact and was felt by the local boys who had their athletic

The old Penetang High School located on Lorne Avenue. It burned to the ground on June 16ᵗʰ, 1962.

To mark her coronation, Queen Elizabeth II bestowed on Sister Mary Lumina a special medal in recognition of her years of service. Presented to her in a special ceremony, Monsignor Castex also brought congratulations on behalf of the parish.

St. Joseph's School was first opened in 1960 and housed English students taught by the Grey Sisters.

and cultural side nurtured by daily contact with them.

As well, the Sisters or Soeurs, made a tremendous impact on their students, the parish and the education of its children. Soeurs Félix had been here since 1935 and in her second year (1937), had received special accolades because 37 of her 51 students had passed provincial entrance exams with flying colours.

In June of 1953, Soeur Marie Lumina, a Grade 8 teacher who specialized in the preparation of students towards their Confirmation, was given a special, commemorative medal by the new Queen, Elizabeth II. The medal, to be worn in honour of the Queen's Coronation, was presented by Monsignor Castex in a ceremony in the Auditorium of Ste Croix.

In 1959, the local school board decided to extend the existing elementary to the secondary panel system in order to provide a Catholic education after grade eight. Since the closing of the Penetanguishene High School to local secondary education, the Penetanguishene students had to be bused to Midland to attend the Midland-Penetanguishene District High School. There was a certain amount of reticence from both parents and students to do that.

For that reason, two grade 9 classes were opened at Ste Croix, with the English one taught by Sister Madeline-de-Sion (Lillian French), and the French one taught by Soeur Roger-de-la-Croix (Jeanne d'Arc Brunelle), originally from Lafontaine.

The parish continued to grow, which necessitated the construction of yet another school, St. Joseph's, which was located across the street from Ste Croix. It opened in 1960. With the rumblings of an impending language war in the town and parish beginning to emerge in the late fifties, it was decided that the English students would best be served by their own school. They moved into the new St. Joseph's taught there by another Order of Sisters - the Grey Sisters of Pembroke, whose Order also ran the General Hospital.

Sister Mary-of-the-Cross was the Principal, joined by Sister Mary-of-the-Assumption, and Sister St. Daniels. They were later joined by Sister St. Bernard.

Fate intervened into Penetanguishene's educational plans in a big way on June 16ᵗʰ, 1962 when the old High School burned to the ground. A new, 21-room school was soon opened near the ruins of the old high school at a cost of $420,000.00. Many thought that this school might end up being the new high school. Gil Robillard recalled the trepidation that the school board felt over the naming of the new school.

" I can recall both sides just waiting for the name to be either French or English, you know, to pounce on it. We tried not to take sides

so we came up with a great name solution - 'Corpus Christi'. When we announced the Latin name everybody was speechless. Nobody could argue with it."

All the Grade 9 and 10 classes, both French and English, were installed on the second floor of the new Corpus Christi School while the bottom floor housed the French grades from Kindergarten to Grade 8. This coincided with the closing of the aging St. Anne's School. Still, there was a secondary education problem in the town and two portables were built behind the church and named "Ecole Secondaire Saints Martyrs Canadiens."

Then in 1962, the parish undertook the building of a small "private" Secondary School near Corpus Christi that would house Grades 11 and 12. Built with a modern look, it had the frontal shape of and was referred to as "the Butterfly School" although its name was "Ecole Secondaire Saints-Martyrs Canadiens" to replace the now defunct portables which had been in use pending the completion of a new building. The difference was that secondary education in this school was supported directly by the parents who had to pay for their child's education in a Catholic school beyond grade 10 in Ontario during that period of time. Unfortunately, the life of this school was short lived, closing in 1964.

Many changes occurred in the public school system here and can be exemplified by a photograph taken in 1964. Where, at one time, the teaching staff would have been

Corpus Christi School, opened in 1962, first housed both secondary classes and French and English elementary classes. It is now called James Keating Public School.

The Butterfly School, opened in 1962, housed Grade 11 and 12 classes. Funded directly by the parents, it lasted only two years.

This 1964 staff picture at Corpus Christi shows the increasing numbers of lay teachers at the school.

predominantly composed of religious orders, this staff picture taken at Corpus Christi School showed 11 Brothers and Sisters teachers while counting 13 lay teachers making up the staff.

In 1964, the last three teaching Brothers and their Superior, Frère Charles, left Penetanguishene for the last time. In their wake, the teaching importance of Sisters was increased. This was best exemplified by the new, modern convent that was opened on Poyntz St. in February of 1964 to accommodate not only the Penetanguishene Sisters but also those from Perkinsfield and Lafontaine who taught in those respective schools. This allowed for the closing down of the convents in the two other communities and centralizing the living accommodations and the costs.

During the 1964-65 school year, the new Penetanguishene Secondary School took over the top floor of Corpus Christi to set up its new school when the Penetanguishene Public School Board decided to close its grades 9 and 10 and the "Butterfly" school closed its doors as well. In 1965, the school board decided to transfer English instruction to Corpus Christi while St. Joseph would accommodate the French students who would now be located across the street from the other French pupils in Ecole Ste Croix. This also suited the Sisters rather nicely, as both these schools were but mere strides away from their residence.

The Grey Sisters transferred with their students up to Corpus Christi. They continued to reside with their Order in the residence beside the General Hospital. Henry Bisschop, a Grade 8 teacher at the time and later Vice Principal at Corpus Christi recalls:

"The last year before she left, Sister Mary-of-the-Cross, the Principal, decided to separate the Grade 8 boys and girls. I had the boys and Sister St. Bernard had the girls across the hall from me. We had a heck of a time that year, because the boys and the girls didn't see each other all day and were at an age when their hormones were kicking in. Let's just say that they were at an age when it was very difficult to keep boys and girls apart for a complete eight hour school day! That was quite a year! As soon as Sister Donelly became Principal in 1968 or 69 we begged and she agreed, to integrate the boys and the girls again. We were thankful for that!"

"What I also remember about the Sisters" continues Bisschop, *"was that they only made 3/4 of the other teachers' salary because they were a non-profit group whose earnings went into their Order and therefore were tax exempt. It used to be so odd at negotiation time."*

It is important to note that, from 1959 through to 1964, while secondary education was being offered locally for Catholic French and English students by the Penetanguishene Public School Board, the newly formed Simcoe County Board of Education was also offering secondary education for all students in the area at the newly built Midland-Penetanguishene District High School, now known as Midland Secondary School.

Lafontaine Continuation School, situated in nearby Lafontaine since 1944, continued to offer Grades 9 to 12 education for Catholic French students as well under the "Soeurs-de-Ste-Croix" located in the village until the new Penetanguishene Secondary

School opened its doors in 1966.

In time, the number of Sisters teaching in Penetanguishene was drastically reduced. In 1968, there were only two Sisters teaching at Ecole Ste Croix, four at Ecole St. Joseph and one at the new Penetanguishene Secondary School, which was opened in the fall of 1966.

Penetanguishene Secondary School

Henry Bisschop recalled the last of the Grey Sisters who left Corpus Christi around 1976:

"When Sister Alicia left, it was the first true sign that public education was becoming more diversified, that the "public" nature of education came to the fore and the religious aspect diminished. I can remember later as Principal when education representatives from Toronto walked through the school and noticed all the crucifixes, remarking that they would have to soon come down. I felt it was a sad time, that the times were a changing! Eventually the school name changed too!"

Despite the changing times the education efforts of the Sisters did not go unrecognized. The work of the "Soeurs-de-Sainte-Croix" was best exemplified when, in 1976, Soeurs Marie-de-S.Eusèbe (Sr. Angéline Moreau), a former Principal of St. Joseph, was bestowed with an Honorary Doctorate from York University for her tireless work on behalf of French-language education.

In her acceptance speech, spoken in impeccable French, she told her academic audience,

"As a French Canadian, I wish that not only in our province, but from one ocean to the other, we could work together, in spite of our different origins, to build a united Canada that is respectful of each person and also, respectful of our two official languages."

In 1985, Soeur Jeannette Quesnelle was the last of the Soeurs-de-Ste.-Croix teaching in the Georgian Bay region. In the 1990s the last of their Order left their convent on Poyntz St. in Penetanguishene. Sadly, it sat empty for a few years before the building with its beautiful chapel was sold to a private developer and converted into a home for the aged.

Soeur Angéline Moreau (Soeur Marie-de-S Eusèbe). Received her Honorary Doctorate of Letters from Glendon College, York University, 1976.

Père Louis Dignard.
10th Pastor of St. Anne's 1969-1993

9

A Gentle Hand of Change

In 1969, when Père Louis Dignard assumed his full responsibilities as the 11th Pastor of St. Anne's Church, he already was fully engrained in the work and management of the parish. He knew North Simcoe very well.

Born on November 26th, 1912 in Port McNicoll, into a family of nine siblings, Louis Dignard grew up around the grain elevators there. His father, the head of a work team who unloaded the grain, also had a farm with pigs and chickens to feed his young family. Sunday family picnics on the point near his home and fishing expeditions with his father were greatly responsible for Louis' love of the outdoors.

Having finished his schooling to grade nine, young Louis took a job with the Canadian Pacific Railroad in Port McNicoll. Recognizing academic potential in the young Dignard, Father Danny McNamara, the mission priest from Midland, persuaded the young man to make an application to "Collège Sacré-Coeur" in Sudbury, as it was offering yearly education packages for $150.00, board and meals included. He applied to the College, and much to his surprise, was accepted.

In his final year of studies where he majored in philosophy, young Louis was again approached by Father McNamara. He urged the young man to enter the seminary to study for the priesthood. "Go for a year," the priest counseled him, "and if you don't like it, then you can leave and go on to be a doctor or lawyer or whatever you feel you'd like to be."

He entered St. Augustine's Seminary in Toronto and came to a gradual conclusion that he wanted to devote his life to the service of

God and his fellow men. He excelled so well at the Seminary, especially in Theology, that his ordination was advanced a year. He was ordained in his hometown church in Port McNicoll by Cardinal McGuigan in 1943.

His first assignment was to Penetanguishene, where he said that, "Monsignor Castex knew that I was bilingual and that was to his advantage. I'm sure he was influential in my getting assigned to him."

Upon his arrival here, in July of 1943, he knew that language tensions already existed in the parish. As a newly-ordained priest under the direction of a strong pro-English Pastor, the fluently bilingual young priest did his best to avoid being caught in the battlefield.

"I was quite at ease and quite comfortable at St. Anne's immediately upon my arrival," Père Dignard recalls, *"and I had made a decision to stay out of the fray. I was with Father Sullivan who could speak French a little bit, and there was also another priest who stayed only a year to help out. Things worked out pretty well. We each had two masses to say on Sundays."*

His first stay lasted almost seven years. But before his new assignment to a new parish could be carried through, he had to be replaced at St. Anne's. This was delayed due to Monsignor Castex's refusal to accept an older, newly-ordained priest from Toronto whom he felt might be unsure as to his true calling. After much delay and pressure from the Chancellery, a replacement finally came through and Père Dignard was re-assigned

in January of 1951. He spent the next thirteen years in Toronto, Pickering, Brechin and Perkinsfield, where he arrived in 1961.

With the moving of Father Kelly from Penetanguishene to the new Seminary, August of 1964 found the soft-spoken, gentle Dignard re-assigned as Assistant Pastor to Monsignor Castex at St. Anne's here in Penetanguishene. It was an assignment that he relished, for it was near his hometown of Port McNicoll. North Simcoe was a place he knew so well. He had always docked his boat in Port McNicoll, which allowed him to explore and enjoy his love of fishing, the water, hunting and nature, which were constant elements throughout his life.

Due to Monsignor Castex's deteriorating health, Père Dignard for all intent and purposes ran the parish, taking over where Father Kelly had left off. In 1969, he was officially but quietly appointed the pastor of St. Anne's.

A special memory of those early years as pastor encompass a special time, that to him, illuminated the meaning of God's love and true charity. He recalls:

"There was a poor family across the bay by the name of Link. They had six girls, from the crawling stage to age six. They had fallen on hard times and were very poor. They had each one dress and the mother would have to wash them and immediately put them back on the girls.

"I mentioned the situation to the Ladies-of-St. Anne's who took that family in, set them up with clothes and a place to stay in town un-

A young Père Louis Dignard, as he appeared between assignments at St. Anne's.

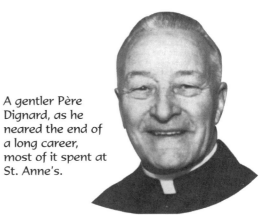

A gentler Père Dignard, as he neared the end of a long career, most of it spent at St. Anne's.

til they could get on their feet, you know, fend for themselves. That was my warmest memory and showed the generosity of God's love. I thought that was really great!"

Father Leonard J. Wall had been coming up to the Penetanguishene area for a long time. Louis Dignard recalls his first contact with a man who would have an influence on his parish during his pastorship:

"I first met Leonard Wall when he would often come up in the summer. He came each summer to help out when Monsignor Castex had the place at Marygrove. He would stay at the rectory, and sometimes went around the bay to Marygrove, have lunch there and then return. He grew to be very fond of St. Anne's. I don't think he missed a summer visit for quite some time. And of course he could golf up here and relax. Len sure loved his golf!"

"During the years he taught at the seminary, Father John Kelly continued to have a cottage up in Penetang at Coutnac Beach," recalls Archbishop Wall still. *"And I would come up with him to stay at his cottage whenever I had a day off. His family used it as well."*

Père Jean Marc Gagné.
Père Gagné returned to being a military chaplain shortly after leaving St. Anne's. As Associate Pastor here between 1964-1968, he was instrumental in rejuvenating the choir.

From 1964 through to 1969, priests sent to assist at St. Anne's included Fathers Drake Will, Brian Clough and Pères Jean-Marc Gagné, Alphonse Robert and F.A. Bernier.

By 1969, when Louis Dignard assumed the charge at St. Anne's, Father Leonard J. Wall, his good friend, who, for many years had been the secretary to Cardinal McGuigan, was now the new Chancellor of the Diocese. No small job. Because of this, there were constant business and personal contacts with his friend "Lou".

In July of 1970, the Chancellor needed some time away, "from the rat race" as he sometimes referred to it, away from his heavy responsibilities in the diocese. His place of rest was no other than Penetanguishene.

On August 4th, 1970, Chancellor Wall wrote a letter to Louis Dignard to discuss the usual church matters of dollars, accounts and balancing the books, but he ended by writing:

"Following the wonderful week of rest in your rectory, I am feeling much better and actually playing golf a little better once again although not often enough. The summer is far from over yet and I certainly hope to be able to come 'home' to Penetang once more."

The following summer he wrote on July 22nd, 1971:

"Dear Lou,

"It seems a strange summer to me not to have been to Penetang by this date. Actually had the Père (Castex) lived through the winter this would have been the day we would have celebrated his 100th birthday even though on the memorial card and on the marker at the cemetery July 23rd is given as the date of his birth. True to his character, there will probably be corrections made into his post-mortem period.

"Rest assured that before too much more of the summer goes by I will be in Penetang for occupancy of the back room and temporary tenancy of the Midland Golf Club."

On Saturday, July 24th, 1971, an old friend of the parish, Athol Murray, now a Monsignor, returned to the town to rededicate and bless "his" angels which had been handsomely placed on two new monuments, marking the entrance to the town. A special platform was erected at the entrance to the town where Père Dignard led the group in prayer before Mayor Vince Moreau introduced the guest of honour. Père Murray did not disappoint the crowd, as he gave a rousing speech praising the bicultural and rich heritage of the town. He was glad and proud to be back. Soloist André Boileau accompanied by Mrs. Marchand, then entertained the crowd.

In 1972, the sanctuary was remodeled according to the liturgical renewal proposed by the Second Vatican Council. The high altar of marble built by Monsignor Castex in 1960 was partly dismantled and moved. The marble tabernacle itself was moved forward and re-incorporated into a new side altar while the marble table with columns and its lighted mosaic tile picture of the "Last Supper" was moved forward to make the new altar table at the centre of the Sanctuary. It was a credit to Père Dignard that none of the original marble altar was lost due to these changes but were masterfully reincorporated into the new design without too much fuss.

Some parishes were not so lucky. Many of them had had their altars and tabernacle donated by certain people or groups in the parish who were still alive and were against "their" altars being tampered with and in some cases, even destroyed. It marked a very stressful time for the universal church and for many of its priests. The changes caught many of them off guard.

"The painters were making alterations to the Sanctuary," recalls Dignard, *"and were about to paint over the angels that used to grace each side of the large crucified Christ at the front of the church where the high altar used to be. I said to them, 'What are you guys doing? Do you have permission to do that?' And they answered that 'Yes, the archdiocese had instructed' them to. I nodded and said 'Oh, well I guess that's ok . . . I guess'."*

It was indeed a time of change and also for the first time, the celebrant priest said mass facing the people, with the whole mass celebrated in the language of the people. The Latin Mass was a thing of the past.

In February of 1974, the parish was abuzz when a

Monsignor Athol Murray addresses the crowd at the re-dedication of the Angels on Saturday, July 24th, 1971. *Courtesy Penetanguishene Centennial Museum.*

parishioner called Père Dignard to perform an "exorcism" in her apartment. Eerily, this coincided with the release of the "Exorcist" movie but the real thing wasn't quite as dramatic. The good pastor simply said a short prayer and sprinkled some holy water about. However, the story made headlines in The Toronto Star.

In the summer of 1975 Penetanguishene celebrated its 100th Birthday of incorporation as a village. Again Père Athol Murray left his beloved University of Notre-Dame in Saskatchewan to come "home" to help us celebrate "Old Home Week". Before arriving, he sent a glowing letter praising the important history of the town and its significance to the country. He wrote words that beckon to us still:

"A great thrill it is to me to see the proud enthusiasm of Penetanguishene in commemorating its past. I assure you that I feel highly honoured to find myself invited to be your guest...

"I have always been obsessed with the conviction that Huronia and particularly Penetanguishene will be recognized as the ultimate nucleus of Canada's identity. The vital thing is to secure its recognition and I feel the community should mobilize all its energies to that objective . . .

"In 1615, Champlain erected a wooden cross at Atouacha. The tradition of that cross was maintained down the years - there was one there in my time . . .

What is there to prevent Penetanguishene

The cross that was at Toanché during Père Murray's time.

erecting an iron cross at Atouacha and installing similar lights (as in Montreal). It would be a great assertion of faith and incidentally something tourists would really go for.

"I'd play up Champlain. The Orillia monument of Champlain and Brébeuf is one of the most beautiful things in Canada . . . That doesn't take away from Penetanguishene; it brings out the salient Huronia fact that Penetanguishene - in the Huronia complex - had priority with Champlain and Brébeuf and still has. Yes, I would play up the Atouacha cross - and Champlain and Brébeuf - and very much Père Joseph LeCaron.

"Next play up the Memorial Church - it has a history unique in Canada. Have the bronze plaque polished up and given a full page. No community in Canada can boast a Church with the history of yours. Only a priest of the mind of Father Laboureau could have engineered it through the Senate of France and the Congress of the United States. I have always felt that the people of the district never contrived to grasp its significance . . ."

It seemed that Père Murray was always thinking of the town and the parish in the grand scale of things. His idea of a great lighted cross at the shore near Toanché was examined but shelved due to a lack of time and money. Despite it all, he visited and kicked off the Centennial parade with a speech in which he reminded residents:

"It's a great thrill to be back in the old town and see you've never lost your love for a

Monsignor Athol Murray walks down the parade route greeting residents. He is supported by Doug Dubeau, Chairman of the town's 1975 Centennial celebrations.

During the 1975 Centennial celebrations, St. Anne's Choir gave an enthusiastic performance at the Pen Theatre that brought the house down.

parade . . . The people of Penetanguishene have a great responsibility to Canada. You're both French and English but you're pals. You're not squabbling like they are in Montreal . . .

"I want to come back some time in the future when you put up a great cross . . . I want to urge you that Penetanguishene . . . Huronia . . . can do a hell'va lot to keep Canada together!"

To show his enthusiasm for the project Murray donated $500.00 towards it. Sadly, it was our last look at the man who died only months later in December of that year. Indeed the whole country mourned his loss.

The Centennial celebrations were a great hit with its many festivities, one of which was a concert put on at the Pen Theatre by St. Anne's Choir. Soloist Vola Carrière wowed the crowd as did André Boileau, who received a standing ovation and was forced to return for an encore.

Mrs. Lucrèce Marchand, the parish's faithful organist for many years, was presented with flowers for her piano accompaniment.

"Mrs. Marchand was a great lady," recalled Louis Dignard. *"She was always available for masses and funerals no matter what, and I can recall her often playing for nothing. She loved to play the organ at the church. I don't know what we would have done without her those many years."*

This same year, the French communities of Penetanguishene and Lafontaine were the subject of filming for a television 26-part documentary series called "Villages et Visages." A project of the Ontario Educational Communications Authority, this first show featured footage of St. Anne's Church and organist Lucrèce Marchand.

On the morning of July 26, 1976, two men in Toronto, Fathers John Kelly and Leonard Wall, had agreed to come up to Penetanguishene. Kelly had complained of

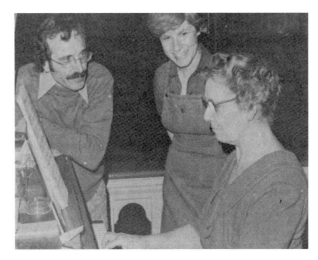

Mme. Lucrèce Marchand being interviewed for the French documentary, "Villages et Visages" while she plays her beloved organ in St. Anne's Church.

not feeling well that morning, so he stayed back while Len Wall drove on up ahead of him. Wall continues:

"That afternoon I phoned John from his cottage and I said that I had had a good siesta and a swim and that I was going to drive in to Penetang and have supper at the rectory. He said he'd come up the next morning.

"That night I decided to stay in town, at the rectory, and slept in the back room when one of the priests woke me up. On the phone was the Rector of the seminary, Father Harold O'Neil, to tell me that John had died that night. I went up to the General Hospital to say Mass for the Sisters and then returned to Toronto."

On August 17th, 1981, Penetanguishene Town Clerk Administrator, Yvon Gagné, informed Pastor Dignard by letter that, Heritage Penetanguishene, a local conservation group and a committee of Council, intended to designate St. Anne's Church as *"an architectural and heritage structure deemed for protection under the Ontario Heritage Act"*.

Interestingly enough, in its reasons for a designation status, Heritage Penetanguishene listed the six chimneys as one of the many special features of the building. The researched document stated:

"The six chimney stacks on the gable roof show a diversion from the true 11th to 13th centuries Romanesque to a more Gothic style. It has been suggested that this could be a characteristic of the 19th century Romanesque. The architect also may have wanted to convey the height established by the front façade, along the 140 foot depth of the building."

As all pastors found out down through the years, this architectural wonder of a church was always in need of upgrading and repair. At one point, the pastor had his brother Frank Dignard repair the lead in some of the stained glass windows. Now, in the fall of 1983, the worry of a new roof and those historic chimneys could not be put off any longer.

"It got that, whenever it rained," Dignard recalls, *"water came down the right wall of the church and on the left where the statue of Our Blessed Lady was. The water would drip on*

her face. I called the chancellery and they said to go ahead and get the problem fixed. We put on a new roof and also had the chimneys fixed and re-pointed.

"The chimneys really needed to be fixed as the smoke often backed up and I was forever finding starlings and bats in the basement."

In 1984, with the approaching visit of Pope John Paul II to the Martyrs' Shrine and St. Marie-Among-the-Hurons, both in Midland, plans began in earnest to redecorate St. Anne's Church. In January, contractor Ted Lenssen of Orillia gave a quote to repaint the interior of the church, clean and restore the canvas paintings, and strip and refinish the church pews.

On February 17th, 1984, a letter arrived from the Vice Chancellor, Father Nick De Angelis, stating:

"I am pleased to inform you that Bishop Wall gladly approved

This 1908 photo, taken only six years after she was officially opened, clearly shows the old church's chimneys and splendid architecture.

works of renovation and repair through the COED Program to your church, as specified . . . not to exceed $34,800.00".

Scaffolding graced the interior and pews were disarranged for many months, but when it was completed, this work truly beautified the interior and brought it to a high standard.

Education in Penetanguishene took many interesting turns in the 1980's and 90's. In the early 80's, the English and French public schools, which until then had been Catholic schools named Corpus Christi, Ste. Croix and St. Joseph became true public schools. Crucifixes and religious teaching were removed. Corpus Christi was renamed James Keating Public School. St. Joseph retained its name but later also lost its crucifixes, religious inferences and teaching. Ste Croix, which had been closed earlier, was now St. Joseph's Annex.

Catholic families in the public schools wishing to maintain religious teaching for their children had to now enroll them in the Catholic school system. This coincided with the growth of the Catholic population of both languages. For the English, St. Ann's Catholic Elementary School was constructed first, with portables near the old Butterfly school on church-owned land, and then next to Penetanguishene Secondary School. École St. Louis was constructed for the French students near parkland past the Brûlé Heights subdivision. Then, Canadian Martyrs Catholic School was opened in the Fall of 2000 and built off Gignac Drive. It took the overflow from St. Ann's School which was growing by leaps and bounds.

The 150th anniversary of the actual establishment of St. Anne's Parish in Penetanguishene was celebrated in 1985. The parish struck up a special Anniversary Committee which was composed of Alvin Gravelle, Ellie Vanden Heuvel, Georgette Bellisle, Terry Keenan, Adrien Lamoureux, Lucille Zoschke, Soeur Priscilla Maurice, Annette Dupuis, Medora DeVillers, Louise Leclaire, Theresa Marchand, Christiane Lavoie and Wayne Rogers.

Pope John Paul II sent a special "Apostolic Blessing" to the parishioners via a large certificate.

St. Ann's School

École St. Louis

This 1985 certificate, sent by His Holiness, Pope John Paul II, marked the parish's 150th anniversary.

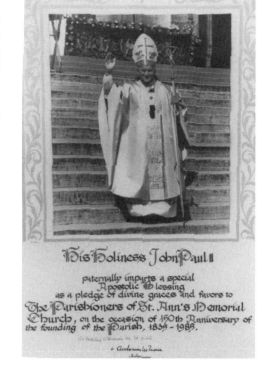

His Holiness John Paul II

paternally imparts a special Apostolic Blessing as a pledge of divine graces and favors to The Parishioners of St. Ann's Memorial Church, on the occasion of 150th Anniversary of the founding of the Parish, 1835 - 1985.

The Archbishop of Toronto, Gerald Emmett Cardinal Carter, sent a letter of congratulations that included the following comments:

"There are very few parishes in the Archdiocese of Toronto who are able to celebrate their one hundred and fiftieth anniversary.

"It is an indication of the profound traditions and the depths of the pioneer faith which planted the seed which has produced so much at St. Anne's. Truly these founders, most of them French-speaking pioneers, were giants of their time and of any time.

"We honour them and we honour all of those who have laboured in this parish over all these years."

Auxiliary Bishop of Toronto, Robert Clune, sent his best wishes in which he stated:

"Before I went to St. Augustine's Seminary in 1938, I had little knowledge of Penetanguishene. But as God would have it, St. Anne's sent a seminarian to St. Augustine's that year as well. His name was Norbert Gignac. The next year Alfred 'Bud' Quesnelle came to the seminary too. Through them, I came to know their families and other friends and to learn of the history and religious traditions of St. Anne's Parish.

"Msgr. Castex was a going concern at that time and we were much impressed by his zeal, initiative and dedication. I came to know . . . that St. Anne's has been blessed from the beginning . . . It is obvious, when one looks at what has been accomplished over the years, that parishioners have responded with enthusiasm and generosity to the teaching and leadership of their priests.

"I do wish to congratulate priests and parishioners of St. Anne's on completing one hundred and fifty years of worship and service as a Catholic Parish community."

And from the Chancellor of the diocese came this short but warm note:

"In celebration of our heritage of faith and our 150 year old history-congratulations. I am happy to be counted a member of the parish family of St. Anne's, Penetanguishene.

Leonard J. Wall"

Emmett Cardinal Carter. He was Archbishop of Toronto at the time of the parish's amazing anniversary.

Auxiliary Bishop of Toronto, Robert Clune.

Bishop Leonard J. Wall. A former "summer appointment", he came back to the parish often to help out and for rest and relaxation from his important job as Chancellor of the Archdiocese.

In 1985, the priests of St. Anne's at the time, Father Richard Jacobson, Pastor Louis Dignard and Father Richard Andrews, posed for this photo.

boasted as being "the largest church north of Toronto and certainly one of the oldest."

Priests who were here between 1985 and 1993 included, Pères Viateur Laurin, Vigny Bellerive, Michel Brochu and Fathers Donald Picone, Duncan McInnes and André Glaba.

In 1993, after fifty years in the priesthood, Père Dignard was fêted for his amazing milestone with a special mass, reception, and dinner. He recalls in typical modest fashion:

"My mass felt like a real parish celebration. What I recall most, was at the dinner afterwards, I approached Sister Camillus, who had done an awful lot for the parish at the General Hospital visiting the sick, the dying, etc. I had her come up to sit at the head table. She says, 'Oh no. That's for important people.' I said, 'Oh yes Sister! You are important people!' She was truly a wonderful lady."

After 24 years at the helm of St. Anne's, (29 years if one counts the first five under Monsignor Castex), he was finally succeeded by Monsignor Leonard O'Malley in 1993. He retired to his new home in

An anniversary photo album of parishioners was put together and in his opening remarks Pastor Louis Dignard wrote this:

"Like the mustard seed of the parable, the seed of faith has grown in Penetanguishene to embrace a large community of several hundred families, . . . May the blessings of Our Lord be with us always."

On November 3rd, 1985, the parish celebrated its 150th anniversary at a special mass celebrated by an old friend who came "home" for the event, Bishop Wall.

Priests who were sent to assist here between 1969 and 1984 were Fathers J.A. DeJonge, Richard Jacobsen, Gordon Davies, Richard Andrews, Joe Harrington, Donald McIsaac and Pères Viateur Laurin, and Justin Desroches.

In 1988, a new heating system was installed and renovations done to Laboureau Hall in the basement of the church. In an article in the local paper, the pastor was obviously proud of his church, which he

Bishop Wall posing with Richard and Frances St. Amant at the reception following the 150th anniversary mass, on November 3rd, 1985.

Port McNicholl. Yet despite his eighty-one years of age at the time, Père Dignard maintained his service to the parish into the new millennium. He continued to say mass each Sunday at the Our Lady-of-the-Rosary Church across the bay.

To show their esteem for his faithfulness to celebrating mass at their Mission church, a special collection was taken by the congregation of Our-Lady-of-the-Rosary, and a reception held for him in St. David's Hall in the basement , when Dignard celebrated his 85th birthday, in November of 1997.

He continued to say mass there without missing a Sunday well past his eighty-seventh year. Then, in the summer of 2000, Père Dignard experienced deteriorating health, which forced him to be hospitalized for an operation. Knowing the feelings and concern his parish still held for their old pastor, Monsignor O'Malley gave weekly updates as to Père Dignard's condition and progress from the pulpit.

Interviewed in Huronia District Hospital in September of 2000, Père Louis Dignard remembered with fondness his years in our midst. The summation of his pastorship was truly symbolic of the man and his quiet humility,

"Time has flown by and memories with it. I really appreciated my time at St. Anne's, its many graces, many converts and many fruitful years. I am thankful to God for these many blessings."

Pastor Louis Dignard
Photo by Michael Odesse

Father Louis Dignard cuts the cake to celebrate his 85th birthday in November of 1997, at a surprise reception in the basement of Our-Lady-of-the-Rosary Church.

Monsignor Leonard O'Malley.
11th Pastor of St. Anne's 1993-

IO

The Finishing Touches...St. Anne's Today

St. Anne's present pastor was born on May 12th, 1935, in Magog, Quebec, near the American state of Vermont. As the second youngest of five boys born to Ken and Alma O'Malley, young Leonard grew to experience farm life. When he was twelve, the family gave up farm life and moved temporarily to Montreal before moving to Oshawa, Ontario. There his father took an assortment of general labourer jobs and his mother continued a 30-year teaching career.

It was here, in late elementary school, where the young boy began to give thoughts of serving people as a priest, thoughts that he put aside until his last year of high school.

"I began to have contact with a young priest named Wilfred Firth, who worked with the youth," recalls O'Malley today. *"One could see how happy he was at doing his work and how dedicated he was. That had a great influence on me and I re-entertained the idea of commencing studies for the priesthood."*

Unsure if he was smart or qualified enough to enter St. Augustine's Seminary, Father Firth encouraged the teenager to try it out. "Go until they kick you out!" the priest advised him. After the third year, Leonard realized that he wasn't going to get kicked out and that the priesthood was his calling. He was ready to say "yes" to God.

On May 28th 1960, Deacon Leonard O'Malley was ordained a priest in St. Michael's Cathedral in Toronto by Bishop Allen, the Auxiliary Bishop to ailing Cardinal McGuigan. His first assignment was a "summer appointment" to St. Anne's Parish in Penetanguuishene under pastor Monsignor Jean-Marie Castex.

At that time, Père Castex spent his summers at the Marygrove

Camp, only coming to town each Sunday morning to say the early seven a.m. mass. The freedom to do ministry was pleasing to the young priest and he quickly saw St. Anne's as a great place to learn. He continues:

"Père Castex was very good at delegating ministry responsibility to his priests. He'd say, 'You do this or handle that', and I must have been doing okay because he'd say, 'Very good, very good! Keep going!'

"St. Anne's Parish was a great place to do ministry with daily masses at the church, the General Hospital which was at 6:30 in the morning, the Convent, the Brother's' house, with added masses on Sundays at St. David's across the bay and the Psychiatric Hospital. There was lots to do."

The other priests here at that time were Pères Louis Bourque, Joseph Marchand and Fathers John Kelly and another "summer" appointment, Leonard Wall, who encouraged young O'Malley's growing interest in golf, taking him out to the fairways with him a few times.

"Father Kelly could not speak French, so Père Marchand and I rotated into those masses and services," O'Malley recalls. *"It was a little confusing for me at first but soon a pattern emerged. The change in schedule was in fact refreshing because we weren't always saying the same mass in the same location. The variety was nice."*

For O'Malley's first two years here, Monsignor Castex stayed at the rectory but ill health forced him to move into the General Hospital after that.

In the summer of 1964, Father Kelly was moved to the new Seminary as its Bursar. His replacement as Assistant Pastor or Apostolic Administrator With Full Power was Père Louis Dignard. That fall, Archbishop Phillip Pocock was visiting the Martyrs' Shrine in Midland and asked to see Father O'Malley, who promptly went to meet with him. There

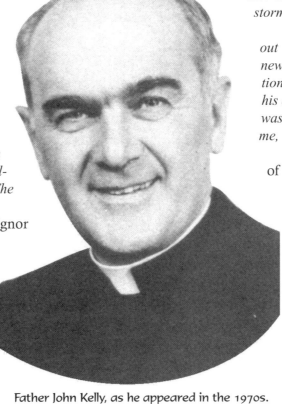

Father John Kelly, as he appeared in the 1970s.

the Archbishop informed him that he was being moved to a new assignment.

Returning to the Rectory, he sat down to a supper later that evening with Père Dignard. O'Malley found his superior very quiet during the meal and his move was not mentioned. Later, in the kitchen as they were doing the dishes, he finally decided to broach the subject of his meeting with the Archbishop and his new assignment. O'Malley told the story to an incredulous Dignard. The latter turned around saying sharply *"What!"* Monsignor O'Malley today recalls the scene as if it was just yesterday:

"Father Dignard was holding a towel in his hand and he threw it into the sink saying angrily, 'They promised me! They promised me! They promised me!' and stormed out of the room.

"It wasn't until some time later that I found out that Father Dignard had initially accepted his new position in charge of St. Anne's on the condition that I be left with him for at least two years as his assistant. It was a great affirmation to me that I was good at what I did and that someone wanted me, that I was valuable."

Reassigned to Brockville in the Archdiocese of Kingston, he was nevertheless reluctant to leave. O'Malley continues,

"You get close to people and a move away can be difficult. You have to uproot yourself and leave people that you have known through happy and sad moments. But, priests are moved in order that they gain more experience to prepare them to one day be in charge of their own parish.

"Perhaps there is a more subtle reason - not every priest appeals to all his parishioners, his moving can be welcomed by some people. There are always personality clashes. Yet, sometimes the move-

ment of a popular priest out of a parish causes pain, and people are hurting. That is understandable.

"It is an imperfect society, but the whole picture evens itself out over a period of time. Remember, even the priest can feel torn about being moved but the new experiences are necessary for him to grow as a priest as well."

Father O'Malley found himself in Brockville for three years, as the chaplain of a hospital during the week and helped on weekends at a small French-speaking community that catered to the relocated employees of a Dupont plant formerly from Montreal. He was moved to St. Mary's Parish in Brampton for a couple of years, before going to St. Ambrose's Parish in the western end of Toronto for another couple of years.

He received his own parish in Barrie when he was assigned to St. Mary's there for the next nine years before being re-assigned to work in the Archdiocese as Director of Priest Personnel for the next nine years. He was given the title of "Monsignor" on June 21st, 1987, following an Investiture Ceremony at St. Michael's Cathedral conducted by the Archbishop of Toronto, Emmett Cardinal Carter.

His Grace, Aloysius Ambrozik,
(Archbishop of Toronto).

Finally in 1993, having asked his superiors for a change from administrative work, the new Archbishop of Toronto, Aloysius Ambrozik held a meeting with him.

"Now, if I asked you to go to St. Anne's in Penetanguishene, what would your reaction be?" the elder churchman asked him.

"I will go tomorrow!" O'Malley answered so fast that the prelate was caught off guard.

"Wait a minute, not so fast. I gather you're open to the assignment?" the soon-to-be-Cardinal asked, smiling.

"Very much so," was the answer. The letter of confirmation arrived shortly after.

And so, twenty-nine years after having left the parish, Monsignor Leonard O'Malley returned as the new pastor of St. Anne's. Prior to his arrival, he had been warned that the Penetanguishene area had high unemployment and was economically impoverished. Upon arriving, he drove around to assess his 'old', new hometown for himself. He was surprised at what he found:

"My first impression was, 'Wow! It has really improved since I had left in '64. I was struck by the beautiful appearance of the homes, the front yards and gardens. The town seemed to have really progressed. It was the exact opposite of what I had expected to see."

But his new task was brought out clearly on his first day with the man he was replacing. He recalls:

"Father Dignard says right off the top, 'Well, the first thing you've got to do is build a new rectory. I had intended to do it but it was a larger project than I was prepared to undertake. And second, you've got to do something about access to the church. Every entrance has steps and older parishioners are finding it more difficult to climb them.'

"I thought, 'Boy, that pretty much fills my plate immediately!!' For the next several years I knew what I would be doing!"

But his next thoughts centered on the man he was replacing. Monsignor O'Malley continues:

"Father Dignard was having a new house built for himself in Port McNicoll, beside his brother Frank's house. So I first welcomed him to stay here in the rectory for as long as he needed. Then, I let him know that while I wanted to respect his retirement, he was still a very valuable and *respected member of St. Anne's and so I asked him if there was something he wanted to do to stay involved in ministry in the parish.*

"He asked to continue to say the Sunday mass at 9:30 at Our-Lady-of-the-Rosary across the bay. He asked that that be all though. He did not want to do funerals or weddings as I think he found them too draining emotionally and he did not want to be put in the position of saying 'yes' to one parishioner and 'no' to somebody else.

"It was extremely helpful to still have him at the rectory for awhile, so I could ask him questions about the parish and things. Access to his knowledge and experience was a godsend. Afterwards, his years of saying the mass at the mission church across the bay certainly helped tremendously as well."

The reception from his new, "old" parish that Monsignor O'Malley received upon his arrival warms him still. People came forward with memories, times and events spent together and at first, he had difficulty putting names with faces, especially when the faces were twenty-nine years older. He found the welcome overwhelming.

He recalled one lady coming up to him with a picture of a wedding long ago. She said to him:

"Monsignor O'Malley, you married my husband and I thirty-two years ago and tomorrow I am so proud that you will be marrying my daughter!" Clearly touched, he couldn't help but laugh and say,

"Oh please, don't make me feel so old!" It was a warm welcome that happened

repeatedly as the parish embraced him.

As his first Christmas here in 1993 approached, O'Malley, deep in thought as to the planning of the rectory, received a visitor to the door that would clearly be a sign of things to come. He continues:

"This guy shows up at the door, an ex-parishioner, proposing or inquiring about raising money for new steeples. He always felt that the church looked unfinished and wanted to rectify the image. I thought the guy was crazy!

"But I wasn't about to say no to such a proposal, so as we spoke, I put just two conditions on the idea. 'First', I said, 'this cannot cost the church or the parish anything. Secondly, the funds for the steeples will NOT be raised in this parish.' I didn't say this to be mean but, I was about to raise substantial funds in the parish to either fix up the old rectory or else build a new one. I had my own parish project to worry about. I told him to think about it.

Father Leonard O'Malley, officiating at the wedding of Yvon and Anne Gagné, in July of 1961.

"So, this fellow leaves and then not long afterwards comes back accepting my conditions and wanting to proceed but is unsure how the project should go forward. I checked with the Archdiocese and told them that I have an offer for a project that I can't refuse but that I am about to embark on my own project and I don't want accusations of money mismanagement between two simultaneous projects."

The diocese suggests that the steeple project be handled by and through them, "in trust". At first leery of such an arrangement and the safe return of the raised funds should the project collapse, the "anonymous donor" agreed to the terms. Before long, diocesan lawyers were contacted by "his" lawyers and the arrangements made. The steeple project had life but clearly its own distinct life. The pastor was doubtful that anything would come of it. Raising funds outside of a parish had never been done before. Besides, out of site and out of mind, Monsignor O'Malley now turned his thoughts to more logical and pressing matters - the rectory.

As 1994 arrived, he invited two contractors to look the old house over and make recommendations. Both came to the conclusion that it would be just as economical to tear it down and to rebuild new.

The Parish Council had been disbanded a few years prior to his arrival but there was a Finance Committee in place. A "Building Committee" emerged comprised of some members of the Finance Committee but chaired by a new but familiar face, Anita Dubeau. The Building Committee also consisted of Floyd Putz, Shirley Bellehumeur, Yvon Gagné, and Monsignor O'Malley, with John Gignac heading up the Fundraising Committee.

The first consideration had been to fix up the old rectory but with its relative costs, existing space and usage limitations, this was quickly ruled out. The next option of buying a house in town and making it the rectory did not work either, as there was no room to put in modern, adequate offices in the old church and besides, accessibility to the priests was best served near or beside the church.

The 1999 St. Anne's Building Committee:
Floyd Putz, Shirley Bellehumeur, Monsignor Leonard O'Malley, Anita Dubeau and Yvon Gagné.

This photo show the elevator addition that was added to the west side of the church. *Photo by Yvon Gagné.*

The decision to build a new rectory was arrived at and the task began. First, the Fundraising Committee had its work cut out for it. From the outset, the parish responded with enthusiasm, both morally and financially. A fundraising campaign soon showed great generosity from the parishioners, especially when former Pastor Louis Dignard himself generously donated twenty-five thousand dollars toward the cause.

The Building Committee met in January of 1998 to begin planning in earnest. Their vision was of a two-story rectory attached to the church with an elevator. When a preliminary budget estimate for the project came in at $550,000.00, Monsignor O'Malley wrote the Chancellor and received permission for a $600,000.00 project. Things fell nicely into place but the road ahead was destined to have a few bumps.

Since St. Anne's Church was a "designated" historical structure, Heritage Penetanguishene, a committee of Town Council, had authority over renovations done to or around it. At a meeting with Heritage in March, preliminary plans to physically connect a new rectory to the old church met with opposition. After many months of meetings, Heritage's many recommendations increased the costs of construction, of which the first one alone - the style of stone to be used on the elevator addition had to match the existing church stone, alone added $72,000.00 to the costs of the elevator addition. Some sub-committee meetings between them and the Church Building Committee became what one could politely call "heated".

After the smoke had cleared, an elevator, which was one of the "raison-d'être" for construction, had to be installed in a 'small addition' on the side of the church.

The construction of a new and "detached" rectory proceeded but it had to be situated back and away from the church, on the western side of the property. Thus the grotto had to be removed to make way. All of this delayed the start of construction and added to the costs.

The final design was clearly not the concept that the Building Committee had wanted from the outset but in the end, compromises were made from both groups in order to come up with a workable solution. Architect Bob Laurin, a member of the parish who worked for Michael McNight Architect Inc. out of Barrie, was hired to come up with the final set of design, construction and tendering drawings.

When Monsignor O'Malley wrote the Chancellor of the Diocese in October of 1998 requesting an increase to the budget of 25% to $750,000.00, the reply from William Broadhurst was full of concern. But he understood the parish's dilemma and recommended to Bishop Meagher that the project be approved and allowed to proceed. It was.

The last hurdles were cleared and tenders called in February of 1999. Next came another shock - the actual tender bids. Of nine tenders submitted, Peake Construction from Barrie came in with the lowest price at $784,390.00. One bid actually came in at over a million dollars!! But those figures were still too high. The committee then had to go back to the drawing board to revise the size of their plans, meet with Heritage Penetanguishene and look at ways that they could make the project affordable.

In May of 1999, the stones fell into place, so to speak, and the proper figures arrived at. Construction began in June of the same year. The large Grotto was taken apart and moved out of the way.

After eight months of construction, Monsignor O'Malley and Fathers Fred Schmidt and Carlos Lopez Jr. moved into the new rectory on Monday, December 20th, 1999. St. Anne's Church now had a new elevator addition as well.

After all was said and done, the total tally of construction of the new rectory and elevator addition topped $906,000.00!

In the meantime, the external steeple fundraising campaign by that anonymous donor or donors, was running its course simultaneously, unknown to the pastor. One day, O'Malley happened to be talking to the Chancellor of the Diocese and asked him if anything had ever come of that fundraising and trust fund for the new steeples. The reply shocked him.

"Oh yes," the Chancellor said. *"Their fund is going up. I believe it is now at the $150,000 mark!"*

"You're kidding?" O'Malley answered, almost floored.

This earlier version of the new steeples clearly showed how the project would enhance and finish Père Laboureau's dream.

"No, I'm not," the Chancellor replied laughing, *"and you can't get your hands on it!"* They both laughed. O'Malley couldn't believe it.

Then in May of 1998, a man knocked on the door of the rectory. O'Malley answered it.

"Hello, my name is Brian Rand," the stranger says. *"I am from Oakville and my company builds cupolas and steeples. I've been hired by an architect and I've been looking your church over to put steeples on it but the bell tower is locked and I have to get up there to do measuring."*

The new rectory, built on the western side of the church, replaced the antiquated house that Père Laboureau had built in 1875. *Photo by Yvon Gagné.*

The pastor then let him up and the builder spent the rest of the day measuring. Months later an engineer hired by this same architect showed up to inspect the towers as well and at that point, the pastor began to realize that the steeple project was perhaps going to fly.

In May of 1999, Brian Rand re-appeared at the rectory with a set of drawings, indicating that they had procured the go-ahead from the architect and the Archdiocese and had actually begun to construct the large spires.

O'Malley asked him if they had received the green light from the Town of Penetanguishene. When Rand answered, *"Oh no, we'll go to them at the last minute for the building permit,"* warning lights went off in the pastor's mind. Recalling the difficulties ensued with Heritage Penetanguishene over the design of the new rectory, he sent the builder immediately to the town.

With a smile, O'Malley recalls the process for the steeples:

"I don't know how often they met with Heritage Penetanguishene but things went smoothly. There was not a single problem. They just rolled on through, getting the okay. I felt kind of out-of-touch with the whole steeple situation but I was thankful that someone else was handling it all. I had my plate full as we were by this time building the new rectory. I was kept abreast of developments with the new spires but always after the fact, which was fine with me."

The anonymous fundraising campaign reached $300,000. The first set of elaborate designs would have cost almost three times that amount so the plans were modified to suit the funds on hand. The project was a definite go and when Brian Rand next saw Monsignor O'Malley in October of 1999, he announced, *"Well, you should have your steeples up by Christmas!"* It was an amazing Christmas present!

Having checked with the archdiocese to ensure everything was for real, it was with great satisfaction, pride and thanksgiving that the pastor informed the congregation of the developments and the gift.

It wasn't long after, that two large steeples and two smaller ones sat on the ground beside the church, waiting for their ascent. The old wooden cupola was removed on Monday, November 30th, 1999, and the four bells taken down. For the first time ever, parishioners could see the historic bells up close, and many took the time to inspect their beauty, even to take pictures of them. Then, the tops of the stone towers themselves were reinforced and strengthened to accommodate the large steeples.

In late November of 1999, the new steeples sat on the ground beside the church, awaiting their ascent to their new home.
Photo by Yvon Gagné

On Friday, December 17th 1999, the second of two new steeples are raised into place.
Photo by Yvon Gagné.

Amid howling winds and frigid temperatures, the steeples were hoisted up into place and fastened securely.

The new steeples clearly seemed a godly deed. Monsignor O'Malley cannot help but gaze at the steeples and smile:

"It was a modern-day miracle. In this day and age, when everyone is so self-centered, for people to be so generous, wanting no praise, is truly astounding!

"The Archdiocese couldn't get over it. They said, 'Here you've got this project you know little about, and how on earth did you raise 300,000 dollars? How did it happen? We have never seen anything like it!' They just couldn't get over it!

"It goes to show that God really is doing the driving. He finds his ways. Both the steeple and expansion projects have been so rewarding."

There was one last hurdle to the steeple project. Plans for the large crosses at the top of each to be lit up at night hit a few snags. The company overseeing the work had to experiment with a few lighting variations before success was achieved. When it was, the sight of the great lighted crosses at night was a sight to behold.

"I can tell you one thing," continues O'Malley with a smile, *"one day, when those light bulbs need changing, I won't be the one climbing to the inside and top on those steeples to change them!"*

At the end of the historical brochure about the church, updated in the summer of 2000, Monsignor O'Malley added these words, *"This completes the work begun by Father Laboureau."*

Anita Dubeau sums up her feelings:

"At the end of the discussions, I was disappointed that the rectory could not be attached but we could not delay any longer. I am still so proud that our priests have a beautiful, modern home that respects each of their privacy. It is great to see that.

"Despite the difficulties, I have immensely enjoyed the committee and my work with it. It has been very rewarding!"

Besides the new rectory and steeples there is still much work to be done. Wendy Maurice and her Garden Committee entered into the picture in the design and planting of a new "Biblical Prayer Garden" situated between the new rectory and the church. Planted in the Jubilee Year 2000, it is intended to add beauty and significance to the

She has been called many things; the Cathedral of the North, the Jewel of Georgian Bay or the Canadian National Shrine.
St. Anne's Jesuit Memorial Church as she looks today.
Photo by Yvon Gagné.

grounds. It is hoped the garden will flower and bloom with the various plants, flowers, shrubs and trees that were symbolic in the Bible and native to Jesus' time. The garden is planted in the shape of a large stylized cross. Future enhancements to the garden may include a bench, arbor or perhaps a gazebo of some type. It is intended to be a place of peace, reflection and prayer.

Also on the Building Committee's agenda is the eventual reconstruction of a mini grotto to replace the larger one that had to be removed to make way for the new rectory.

Despite the fact that his official 40th Anniversary of ordination to the priesthood oc-

Wendy Maurice, pictured in the biblical garden, in the fall of 2000.

curred in May of 2000, the Knights of Columbus wanted to have a dinner to help Monsignor O'Malley celebrate the milestone. His seminary classmates had held many celebrations throughout that spring and summer of 2000 and so it was decided that the Fall would be a better time. With his customary humility, he wondered aloud to those around him whether it was a good idea. *"Who would want to come to a dinner for me?"* he asked.

On Saturday, October 28th, he got his answer, as over one hundred and fifty parishioners packed the Knights of Columbus Hall to honour him. In fact, the dinner tickets were scooped up so quickly that many more could have been sold had the hall been larger to accommodate them.

Former associates showed up for the occasion such as Père Michel Brochu, Vice Chancellor of the diocese, who brought greetings from the Archbishop of Toronto, Cardinal Ambrozik, and fellow priests of the diocese. Father Alex Varga returned and spoke to the crowd of his months spent here at St. Anne's and Monsignor O'Malley's influence on him. Also in attendance was Père Gerard Pilon, and Fathers Fred Schmid, and Carlos Lopez. Also making a brief appear-

Former assistants Père Michel Brochu and Father Alex Varga, returned to help Monsignor O'Malley celebrate his 40th anniversary in the priesthood.

ance was the former pastor, Louis Dignard, whose recovery from recent surgery had weakened him considerably.

Monsignor O'Malley received many gifts and speakers roasted him about his golf game and their memories of him. At his turn at the rostrum the guest of honour spoke movingly of his association with Père Dignard and his affirmation of his work with him and returning to a parish as pastor, of which he always held fond memories. He spoke of his close working relationship with various religious orders over the past forty years and the pleasure he takes in being associated with this parish of St. Anne's. He thanked everyone for a great night.

Father Fred Schmidt, Monsignor Leonard O'Malley and Father Carlos Lopez Jr. in Januray, 2001.

In reality, a parish is not a building or even a group of priests with a building. It is a group of people who come together in worship, who aid in worship and help others in a Christian way.

The parish family of St. Anne's is very diverse, engaging, supportive and all have a role to play. They include; church secretaries; housekeepers; custodians; Altar Servers; the Building Committee; the Cenacle Group; Daughters of Isabella; Folk Choirs; Knights of Columbus; Ladies of St. Anne's; Lectors; Ministers of Communion at Church; Ministers of Communion to the Sick; Polyphonic Choir; Prayer Group; Quilting Ladies; Sacristans; Screening Committee; Society of St. Vincent de Paul; and Ushers.

Of such a large family, space constraints us to a glimpse at but a few of them.

André Boileau has been the soloist at St. Anne's for over thirty-seven years. Originally from Timmins, Ontario, Boileau moved here in 1958 but did not begin singing until Père Jean Marc Gagné talked of resurrecting the church choir shortly after his arrival in 1964. He recalls:

"Shortly after he arrived, I met Père Jean Marc Gagné through Père Guy Hamel. Père Gagné wanted to revive the choir especially for the upcoming Midnight Mass. He asked me if I sang. I had come from a family of singers. Many of my brothers and sisters have beautiful voices. I sang bass and that was what the choir here really needed.

"But I also played Sunday morning hockey in the Rec league, which did not coincide with Sunday morning mass, you know, to sing with the choir. Père Gagné asked how much I wanted for my skates! He wanted to buy them so that I would instead join the choir, which I did end up doing. So instead of going home to Timmins to sing with my family that Midnight Mass like I had always done, I stayed here and sang that Christmas of 1964, and for the next twelve or thirteen Christmases after that in a row."

The soloist for funerals at St. Anne's for many years had been Andy Vaillancourt followed by Lionel Lortie. Lortie, who worked for the school board in Barrie, found it increasingly difficult to get away from work to sing at funerals and was finally forced to give this up in 1967. André Boileau continues:

"Père Gagné comes to me and asks if I could sing at funerals for a few months until they could find a replacement. I was doing bodywork on cars with Celestin Dupuis on Robert Street. His house and shop were near the church and he didn't mind and so I agreed for a few months.

"Well it wasn't long that I was singing all the time. I don't think they ever looked for somebody else. After he had been moved to another parish and to this day, when I see Père Gagné, I ask him if he has found my replacement yet! We have a good laugh about it!

"But during those years when we were with Père Gagné and then Father Brian Clough, who really knew his music, we had great times and a great choir. There were twenty to twenty-five of us and I am sure that we will all say that those days, the days of 'la vieille chorale', were the best times. The leader makes the choir and those two priests were godsends. Even after he had been moved to another parish in 1969, Father Clough would drive up from Toronto once a week to help the choir practice, to keep it going! He was amazing."

André Boileau

Organists have always played a big part of life at St. Anne's. Phil Montgrain played for many years and Lucrèce Marchand played for many decades until her retirement in 1986. She was followed by Germaine Lespérance, and Caroline Crawford. Patricia MacNamara presently does most of the accompaniment with Boileau at weddings and funerals.

St. Anne's has always had a choir in one form or another. In the late 1980s the present choir was given new life under the tutelage of Father Vigny Bellerive. Composed of approximately 25 members of various ages, the bilingual choir sings intermittently at the French and English mass each Sunday. On special occasions they perform in Latin as well. Their Christmas Concert is the group's highlight of each year's performances and activities.

Michelle Quealey has been the organist for the St. Anne's Polyphonic Choir, as they are now known since 1990. She says the group takes its role seriously:

"We are a group of people that carry on a great tradition of choirs here at St. Anne's. We are devoted to providing the best music we can to help with the mass and the liturgy - and we also have fun while we're doing it! We all enjoy it very much!"

Lecturer Lucille Robillard has been reading at masses at St. Anne's since 1984. As one of almost two dozen readers who read French and English, she fully enjoys her participation on the Sundays she is scheduled to read:

"I truly enjoy reading for the Grace of God, keeping and taking part in our Christian worship and community. I look forward to taking an active role. I believe it is important for people to take part!"

Ushers have always played an active and visible role during the masses over the years. Montfort Pilon had been Head Usher for 30 years. Marcel Duval, another former Head Usher, has been a volunteer at St. Anne's since he served in the Second World War. As one of 45 or so ushers, led now by Léo Desjardins, who has also been an usher close to a half century himself, Duval looks back fondly on over 52 years of greeting people, taking the collections, or just being around to help during mass:

"I've always enjoyed working for the church and being

St. Anne's Polyphonic Choir

This small statue of St. Anne and a young Mary is present at all meetings of the Ladies of St Anne's.

around the church. As a 4ᵗʰ Degree Knight, I also help at funerals and ceremonies and stuff. It's just something I've always done, and I've truly enjoyed it!"

The Ladies of St. Anne's, led by Lucille Zoschke, play an important fundraising role in the parish. With an active group of seventy-five ladies out of approximately a two-hundred membership, the Ladies raise funds for the parish and other charitable foundations. Zoschke explains:

"The Ladies of St. Anne's do everything from raffles, bazaars, luncheons, rummage sales and quilting to raising funds for the church and other groups. We do cake and tea at confirmations and special parish functions and receptions. We are always doing one project or another. And we're growing!"

The Knights of Columbus were estab-

lished in the parish in 1912 but lagged during the Second World War. Monsignor Castex revived the group in 1949 and they have been going strongly ever since. In fact they serve five churches in the area: St. Anne's and its mission church; Our Lady of the Rosary; Thunder Bay; Ste Croix in Lafontaine and St. Patrick's in Perkinsfield. The group's primary activity is to fundraise for the parish but also they give monies to the sick, the youth and the needy in the community. The 4ᵗʰ Degree Knights help at all funerals and provide Honour Guards at special masses and occasions.

"We like to be involved in the parish and the church, like helping at funerals," states Grand Knight Art Beausoleil. *"We have helped with parish fundraising for capital projects which is our first priority really, but we also like to help at other things in the community."*

A parish would also not be a parish if it did not attract some of its citizens to serve God in a more direct way through religious vocations such as the priesthood or as Sisters and Brothers.

Gérald Lahaie entered the Jesuit order after 1921.

James Sylvester "Sid" Howe was born in Penetanguishene on February 12ᵗʰ, 1912 and was ordained on June 11ᵗʰ, 1938 at St. Michael's Cathedral in Toronto. He retired in 1982 and died on July 18ᵗʰ, 1998 in Picton, Ont.

Huronia Council 1627
Msgr. Castex Assembly

CHURCH, CHARITY, COUNTRY!

Norbert Gignac was ordained by Cardinal McGuigan at St. Michael's Cathedral in Toronto on May 26th, 1945. He retired in 1996 and presently resides in Thornhill.

Alfred "Bud" Quesnelle was ordained on June 8th, 1946, at St. Michael's Cathedral in Toronto by Cardinal McGuigan as well. He retired in 1992 and presently lives in Toronto.

More recently Gérard Pilon was born in Penetanguishene on October 17th, 1961.

Père Gérard Pilon. Originally from Penetanguishene, his first assignment was home at St. Anne's between 1994-1996.

He was ordained on May 14th, 1994 at St. Michael's Cathedral by Archbishop Ambrozik and immediately served here in his home parish for two years before being transferred to St. Patrick's in Perkinsfield. He recalls his first two years as a priest:

"At first, I thought that it would be difficult or awkward, to be a priest with my family in the pews, you know. But in fact it went very well. It was nice. I enjoyed my two years at St. Anne's with Monsignor O'Malley. It felt like home. It was home!"

The exterior beauty and dominance of St. Anne's Jesuit Memorial Church has always attracted artists, tourists and photographers down through the years. Every pastor can relate to visitors being awed by its beauty. Though the church has never been fully marketed by the town as a tourist stop, many paintings and drawings have been done of her over the years. Her beauty clearly draws the artist to reproduce it on canvas or paper. Artist Del Taylor was not prepared for what he saw when he first stepped into the church:

"As an artist, I marvelled at the size and majesty of the exterior of the church but I was filled with a complete sense of wonder when I first walked in.

"The artwork in St. Anne's is on par with some of the greatest pieces that I have personally ever seen! The various forms (statues, windows, murals, marble work and pillars) in all their diversity are not only dynamic but in a class all of their own! I was in complete awe! I had no idea we had such a treasure in this community. It was absolutely stunning!"

This 1982 drawing of St. Anne's by Father Stephen Somerville graced the parish's 150th Anniversary Album.

This 1995 painting by Kathleen Caygill clearly shows the Church overlooking the town.

This 1999 sketch by Ken Hancock was used by Heritage Penetanguishene for its brochure of town-designated heritage sites.

Many have often wondered why such a grand church, intended to be a Shrine in the beginning by her builder, never realized its title or significance. Archbishop Wall sums up his thoughts about this riddle:

"The beauty and architecture of St. Anne's Church is absolutely stunning and, in terms of geography, it has the most prime position in the whole town. It is a grand landmark, especially from the bay. Successive pastors have decorated it with beautiful paintings and religious symbolism.

"It may have been in grandeur and stature a magnificent building and would have been a 'Shrine' of sorts. The Martyrs certainly were there, living in and walking the lands of Penetanguishene and Lafontaine, etc.

"But I believe that the Church of St. Anne's was and became increasingly a 'parish' church. A Shrine is in Midland perhaps because the Martyrs themselves as a group related more closely to Ste. Marie. St. Anne's was and is a parish church.

"But having said that, St. Anne's Church is a very beautiful, grand, even stunning church, both inside and out. And the parish itself certainly has a full and illustrious history."

So as Monsignor O'Malley continues as pastor of St. Anne's here in Penetanguishene, he does so with a bittersweet feeling as he reflects on the past and the future. He can often be found walking around or sitting on the front steps of the church, watching the busy world pass by.

"I am thankful to be here at St. Anne's. I have always been so impressed by the support of the people for one another in the town and the parish. At funerals, people who are not of the Catholic faith come to support the family at the mass, the funeral and it's beautiful to see.

"I find weddings here amazing. I have been in the city where a few people come to the actual wedding but an overwhelming majority go just to the reception and skip the religious part. But here, I find a great majority of the people attend the church service itself, which is the most important part really, and I think it means a lot to the couple getting married. It's good to see the people at the church, even non-Catholics and it's wonderful! It's nice to note that that has never changed in the years since my return.

"I continue to be thankful for a beautiful church and a warm, giving, generous and faithful parish and community. When I look at the new steeples now, for example, I am of the thought that Père Laboureau must now be happy with what he had started. So you see, they were not my project. I merely did what he would have done had he had the finances and the things necessary at the time to finish the church, his church.

"In the end, I think that is what St. Anne's parish is all about- giving and helping. That is St. Anne's."

Indeed. May she be here forever!

Amen!

This 2000 painting by Del Taylor takes symbolic and visionary license with the arrival of Père Jean de Brébeuf on Penetanguishene Bay in 1626.

This impressive 1998 sketch of St. Anne's by Mark Tumber can be seen at www.marktumber.com

Bibliography

Bayfield, John, and Carole Gerow. *This Was Yesterday*. Town of Penetanguishene. 1982

Bériault, Soeur Hélène. *Les Soeurs de Sainte-Croix*. Cornwall: Soeurs de Sainte-Croix, 1989.

Delaney, Paul J., and Andrew D. Nicholls. *After the Fire*. Elmvale. East Georgian Bay Historical Foundation. 1989.

Dupuis, David. *Welcome to the Place of the White Rolling Sands*. Penetanguishene, 1989.
     — *Welcome to the Martyrs Shrine*. Penetanguishene, 1990.

Marchildon, Daniel. *La Huronie*. Ottawa: C.F.O.R.P. 1984.

Parish of St. Anne's. *Along The Bay*. Penetanguishene, 1949.

Parish of St. Margaret's. *Centennial of St. Margaret's Parish*. Midland, 1983.

Paroisse de Lafontaine. *Sainte-Croix de Lafontaine. 1855-1955*. Lafontaine, 1955.

Paroisse de Sainte-Patrick. *Le Bon Dieu est Bon*. Perkinsfield, 1984.

DEL TAYLOR, is a storyteller, historical interpreter, birch bark canoe builder and artist. He attended the Ontario College of Art and has had numerous exhibitions of his work throughout the province. His work hangs in many public and private collections. He painted the artwork for David Dupuis' recent book, *Kitche-uwa'ne' - A Legend*. He is originally from the Curve Lake Indian Reserve north of Peterborough, Ontario. He now resides in Midland, Ontario with his family and works at Sainte Marie among the Hurons.

DAVID DUPUIS, is a nurse, journalist, historian and author. His previous books include; *Kitche-uwa'ne' - A Legend* which he produced with Del Taylor, the internationally acclaimed biography *Sawchuk: The Troubles and Triumphs of the World's Greatest Goalie, Welcome to the Place of the White Rolling Sands, Welcome to the Martyrs Shrine* and was a contributing author to the book about Cognashene, Ontario, *Wind, Water, Rock and Sky*. He and his family are members of St. Anne's Parish in Penetanguishene, Ontario.

MICHAEL ODESSE, a local photographer, is internationally published with his images appearing in magazines and CDs such as National Geographic, Time, Cottage Life, Professional Photographers of Canada and Readers Digest. He has been involved in 3 hardcover books of which two became Canadian Best Sellers.